Place, Void, and Eternity

Place, Void, and Eternity

Philoponus: Corollaries on Place and Void
Translated by David Furley

with

Simplicius: Against Philoponus on
the Eternity of the World
Translated by Christian Wildberg

Cornell University Press

Ithaca, New York

First published 1991 Cornell University Press.

Published in Great Britain and the United Kingdom under the title
Philoponus: Corollaries on Place and Void

Library of Congress Cataloging-in-Publication Data

Place, void, and eternity.
      p.   cm. — (Ancient commentators on Aristotle
   Includes bibliographical references and index.
   Contents: Philoponus, Corollaries on place and void / translated
   by David Furley — Simplicius, Against Philoponus on the eternity of
   the world / translated by Christian Wildberg.
   ISBN 0-8014-2634-0
   1. Aristotle.   2. Place (Philosophy)—History.   3. Philoponus,
   John, 6th cent.   4. Eternal return—History.   5. Science—
   Philosophy—History.   I. Philoponus, John, 6th cent. Corollaries
   on place and void.   English. 1991.   II. Simplicius, of Cilicia.
   Against Philoponus on the eternity of the world.   English.   1991.
   III. Furley, David J.   IV. Wildberg, Christian.   V. Series.
   B485.P52   1991
   114—dc20   90-23732

Acknowledgments

The present translations have been made possible by generous and imagina-
tive funding from the following sources: the National Endowment for the
Humanities, Division of Research Programs, an independent federal agency
of the USA; the Leverhulme Trust; the British Academy; the Jowett Copy-
right Trustees; the Royal Society (UK); Centro Internazionale A. Beltrame di
Storia dello Spazio e del Tempo (Padua); Mario Mignucci; Liverpool University. We further wish to thank Malcolm Schofield, David Sedley and Lucas
Siorvanes for their comments on the translation by David Furley.

Printed in Great Britain

Contents

Preface

This volume makes available in translation two important contributions to the Philosophy of Science by John Philoponus, the sixth-century Christian Neoplatonist. The second treatise, however, survives only in the excerpts provided, together with hostile comments, by his arch-adversary, the pagan Neoplatonist Simplicius.

In the Corollaries on Place and Void, Philoponus attacks Aristotle's two-dimensional conception of place, from which the Greeks, unlike the Latin Middle Ages, freed themselves. Instead, Philoponus supports a conception, more familiar to us, of space as three-dimensional, inert and capable of being conceived as void. His denial that velocity in the void would be infinite, or that speed of fall is proportional to weight, are anticipations, the second greatly to be surpassed, but the first explicitly acknowledged, by Galileo.

In Simplicius *Against Philoponus on the Eternity of the World*, Philoponus emerges as putting his philosophy at the service of Christianity. Exploiting Aristotle's concession that the world contains only finite power, he argues against the pagan that it will not last eternally.

An earlier treatise by Philoponus, also fragmentary, was translated by Christian Wildberg in the present series as Philoponus: *Against Aristotle on the Eternity of the World*.

PHILOPONUS

Corollaries on Place and Void

translated by
David Furley

Introduction

Richard Sorabji

The Corollaries on Place and Void, with which Philoponus interrupts his commentary on Aristotle's *Physics*, are two documents of major importance in the history of science. We think of space as three-dimensional. But Aristotle had denied there was such a thing as three-dimensional space. The nearest equivalent is the place of a thing, which he defines as the two-dimensional surface of its immediate surroundings. This definition, which captivated the later middle ages,[1] never gained much ground with the ancient Greeks. Aristotle's immediate successor, Theophrastus, assembled doubts about it and the next head of his school, Strato, rejected it. Philoponus reports various objections and, along with his contemporary Simplicius,[2] gives them their fullest development.

He himself defines place or space in a more familiar way as an immobile three-dimensional extension which, so far as its own definition is concerned, is empty of body. He does not think it ever is empty in fact, or even can be empty, any more than matter can exist without form. But on the other hand, he defends the use of thought experiments involving the impossible. If *per impossibile* the cosmic layers of earth, water, air and fire were not there, what would remain beneath the heavens would be this same extension empty of

[1] E. Grant, 'The medieval doctrine of place: some fundamental problems and solutions', in A. Maierù and A. Paravicini Bagliani, *Studi sul XIV secolo in memoria di Anneliese Maier*, Rome 1981.

[2] Simplicius' *Corollary on Place*, from his *in Phys.*, translated by J.O. Urmson, with notes by Philippe Hoffmann, London and Ithaca N.Y., forthcoming.

body.[3] That the extension never is empty in fact is shown partly by nature's abhorrence of a vacuum which he cites, though he refers to it rather as the force of void, or the risk of void.

One of Aristotle's ideas about place is that it is not inert, but has power (*dunamis*),[4] helping to explain the motion of the four elements, earth, air, fire and water, towards their respective parts of the cosmos. He may mean, although he does not say, that it helps to explain this motion as a final cause or goal. Like Theophrastus, Philoponus replies by comparing the cosmos with an organism. A head craned sideways does not return to its position because of the power of some external place, much less if that place is considered in Aristotle's way as a mere surface. It returns in order to resume its proper relation to the other parts of the body. Similarly, fire rises and clods of earth fall down, not under the attraction of any surface, but in order that they may assume the right relationship to the other elemental bodies. It is the relationship of bodily parts, not space, that has explanatory power. Only Philoponus adds his peculiarly Christian idea that this relationship was bestowed on the elements by God at the time of the Creation.[5] Elsewhere in his commentary, Philoponus points out that his view would allow him to explain elemental motion even in a vacuum.[6]

Most of Aristotle's arguments against the possibility of vacuum focus on one particular issue – the impossibility of motion in a vacuum. This was a riposte to those opponents whose chief motive in postulating a vacuum was precisely to allow room for motion. The most influential of Philoponus' arguments in the Corollaries were those which defended the idea of motion in a vacuum. It was not that he thought a vacuum possible, but if *per impossibile* there were a vacuum, there would be no obstacle to motion in it.

Aristotle had complained in effect that, in the absence of any resistance, speed would, absurdly, become infinite. Philoponus replies that there must be something wrong with

[3] Philoponus 574,13ff.
[4] Aristotle *Phys.* 4.1, 208b11.
[5] Philoponus 579,27-580,3; 581,18-31.
[6] Philoponus 632,4-634,2.

Aristotle's view, because, on their shared geocentric hypothesis, the rotating heavens are not surrounded by anything, so encounter no resistance, yet have a finite speed of rotation.[7] The error is this: all motion takes time. What you would achieve by removing resistance is not the necessity for time, but the necessity for *extra* time spent in overcoming resistance.[8] Both the *extra* time argument and the argument about the speed of celestial rotation were passed on through the Arabic philosopher Avempace (Ibn Bajja), and were known, for example, to Averroes and Thomas Aquinas, who attempt various replies, although Thomas accepts the extra time argument. Accordingly, Galileo acknowledges both Philoponus and Thomas as recognising finite velocity in a vacuum.[9]

Philoponus examines the details of Aristotle's argument. If Aristotle were right that for a given weight of body the speed of fall varies in direct proportion to the density of the medium, then it would be plausible that for a given medium the speed of fall would vary in direct proportion to the weight. But this can be measured and seen false by observation: if you double the weight and drop it from the same height, it will not fall twice as fast.[10] Evidently someone had anticipated the experiments which used romantically to be ascribed to Galileo's activities from the top of the leaning tower of Pisa. But Philoponus does not go quite as far as Galileo, because he does not think that the speed would actually be exactly the same.

Not quite all of Philoponus' defence of motion in a vacuum is included in the Corollaries: his most important idea is to be found in the main commentary instead. Aristotle had distinguished unnatural motion as being due to an *external* cause that maintains contact with the moving body. The question then arises how a projectile continues to move after it is parted from the most obvious such external cause – the

[7] Philoponus 690,34-691,5.

[8] Philoponus 681,17-30.

[9] The historical details are summarised in Richard Sorabji, *Matter, Space and Motion*, London and Ithaca N.Y. 1988, 146-8; 283-4. Further details can be found both in this book and in Richard Sorabji (ed.), *Philoponus and the Rejection of Aristotelian Science*, London and Ithaca N.Y. 1987, chs 1 (Sorabji), 4 (Wolff), 5 (Zimmermann), 6 (Furley), 7 (Sedley), 12 (Schmitt).

[10] Philoponus 683,5-25.

bowstring, or the hand of the thrower. Aristotle's answer is that a succession of pockets of air receive from the thrower the power to move the projectile onwards, even though they themselves are no longer being moved. It is then an objection to projectile motion in a vacuum that a vacuum would not contain the air which has this marvellous power of acting as a no longer moved mover.

Philoponus' reply involves what Thomas Kuhn has called a scientific revolution, or paradigm shift.[11] He introduces the idea of an impetus, or impressed force, which is implanted from outside, not into the pockets of air, but directly into the projectile itself. This idea, transmitted perhaps through Ghazali, and taken up in the Latin West, was a commonplace by the time of Galileo. It was not superseded until the idea of inertia was accepted, the idea that no force at all is needed to explain continuing uniform motion in a straight line. It is simply a basic law that motion tends so to continue, unless a force acts on it to the contrary. Impetus and inertia alike can both answer Aristotle's question how projectile motion could continue in a vacuum, and Philoponus uses his impetus to explain both that[12] and Aristotle's further question why a projectile should in a vacuum stop here rather than there: it would stop when the impetus was exhausted.[13] The commentary on *Physics* Book 4 thus complements the Corollaries, but the main arguments are assembled here.

---

[11] Thomas Kuhn, *The Structure of Scientific Revolutions*, Chicago 1962, ᵈ ed 1970, 120.
[12] Philoponus 641,13-642,20.
[13] Philoponus 644,16-22.

PHILOPONUS

Corollaries on Place and Void

Translation

Translator's Note

In book 4 of his *Physics*, Aristotle analyses the concept of *place*. We need this concept, he says, for two reasons. We want to be able to give an account of locomotion – that is, of the movement of a thing from one place to another. Secondly, we need a frame within which to view the observed motions of the four elements: earth and water tend to move downwards, air and fire upwards.

Philoponus' 'Corollary', marked *'parekbasis'* in the margin of the Marcian manuscript, follows a relatively brief set of comments explaining without criticism a passage of the fourth chapter of book 4, 211b5-212a7.

In that passage, Aristotle suggests four candidates for identification as the place of a body:

(a) its form;
(b) its matter;
(c) the extension contained by its boundaries;
(d) those boundaries themselves.

He dismisses (a) briefly in 212b12-14: form belongs to the body itself, but place belongs to the body's surroundings. A similar objection, in 211b36, refutes (b). His strategy is to dismiss (c) also, and therefore to accept (d) as the remaining possibility, now changing the description to read 'the boundary of the containing body' (212a6).

Philoponus, in his reply, first offers criticisms of Aristotle's arguments against (c), then criticises Aristotle's candidate (d), and finally defends (c) with arguments of his own.

14

John Philoponus: Corollary on Place

Commentary on Aristotle's *Physics* pp. 557-85

Now it is time that our own contributions be added to our account, and we spend some time examining whether there is any necessary force in the Aristotelian arguments showing 557,10 that it is impossible for place to be an extension in three dimensions.

I. Critique of Aristotle's argument that place cannot be a three-dimensional extension

(a) Aristotle's First Objection
(*Physics* 4.4, 211b19-23)[1]

To think that place, if it is an extension, penetrates through the whole of the body that comes to be in it, and secondly that it also divides it in such a way as to make an actual infinity of parts, and that the place itself is actually divided to infinity – this seems to me quite foolish and not even plausible.

For if, when they said place is extended in three 15 dimensions, they meant that it is also a body,[2] even then these absurd consequences would perhaps not follow, although

---

[1] Aristotle *Physics* 4.4, 211b19-23. The objection runs like this, in the translation of Edward Hussey (Clarendon Aristotle Series, 1983): 'If there were some extension which was what was naturally [there] and static, then there would be infinitely many places in the same spot. For, when the water and the air change position, all the parts will do the same thing in the whole as all the water does in the vessel.' Hussey (see his note on p. 115) adopts the same text as Philoponus (549,1-4 and 553,1-4), reading as follows in 211b19-20: *ei de ên ti diastêma to pephukos kai menon.* Ross's Oxford text reads: *ei de ên ti [to] diastêma <kath' hau>to pephukos <einai>.*

This is apparently a description of what happens when a pitcher full of water is moved so that the water tips out and is replaced by air.

[2] 'They' means 'those who, like Philoponus himself, hold the view that place is an extension'.

nevertheless the paralogism would have some seductive power. But since they do not suppose place is a body (for they do not claim that to be extended is the same as to be a body), but bodiless (for by its own definition it is void)[3] what
20 necessity is there either that the void must pass into the body that is placed in it, or that it must automatically and in actuality divide the body if it does so pass through it? When it passed through the void, the body just filled it. Furthermore, if the void passed through the body, what kind of necessity was there that it must at once divide it, since it is bodiless? For something bodiless, passing through a body, makes no division or cut in it. At least, whiteness and heat and all the
25 other qualities passing right through the whole of any body (I mean depth and breadth and length) make no division in it, and this is not because they are qualities but because they are bodiless. Body is not of such a nature as to be divided by the bodiless.

If they say, 'But the void is an extension, and therefore it will divide,' even so I see no necessity in it. For even if it is
30 extended in three dimensions, nevertheless it is totally inert and bodiless and just nothing other than empty space. Now,
558,1 how can what is wholly inert and created[4] without any bodily quality, hardness or softness or resistance of any kind or any other power, make a division in bodies? A surface, applied to a surface, makes no division in it; indeed, even if ten thousand surfaces are applied to each other, they do not bring about any
5 increase, nor divide each other, and similarly, if ten thousand lines are applied to each other, they do not make any division in each other or any increase, but ten thousand are able to be applied to each other in the same place (and this for no other reason than that they are bodiless). Just so, obviously, a three-dimensional extension, being bodiless, applied to a
10 three-dimensional one will produce no division nor any other effect whatever.[5]

[3] This does not mean that place is defined as being void (a place may of course be filled), but that if there were a place that was nothing but a place, it would be void.

[4] Reading *pepoiêmenon* for *pepoiêmenôn*.

[5] In Euclid there is a difference between the active and passive use of the verb *epharmozein*: see Sir Thomas L. Heath, *Euclid in Greek, Book I*, Cambridge 1920, 153-4. In the active it is used intransitively (as here) to mean 'to fit exactly', 'to coincide with'. In the passive, it means 'to be applied to' without the implication that the applied figure fits exactly. Philoponus uses active and passive indiscriminately,

Furthermore, if that which is extended in three dimensions, being bodiless and passing through a body – which is the same as to say, applied to the body – divides it, then of course the same will follow for Aristotle's theory also. For he means the place to be equal to what is in the place, and he wants the boundary of the container and of the contained to coincide [literally 'to be in the same']; now if the two boundaries coincide, then the part is in the part as the whole is in the whole. So, since every magnitude is divisible ad infinitum, it will follow that the parts of the surfaces are actually infinite. For if each part of the one surface is not applied to each part of the other one, neither will the whole be applied to whole. So the infinity will be in actuality. I am not saying that one surface will be in the other as in a place: even if it is not as in a place, nevertheless they are applied to each other, and inasmuch as they are applied to each other, they pass through each other, so that they will divide each other. Either, then, it is not possible for a line to be applied to a line, or a surface to a surface, or, if it is possible, then why cannot a three-dimensional extension also, if it is bodiless, be applied to a three-dimensional one? What irrational lottery decided that a length can be applied to a length and a breadth to a breadth, all being bodiless, but a depth cannot be applied to a depth? Yet length and breadth are not without body, but have their being in body; all the same, they are applied to their likes because they themselves are bodiless. But the extension that forms place is bodiless and separable from body and self-subsistent, not having its being in a substrate.[6] All the more, then, will it be able to be applied to the body and leave it unaffected.[7] For if the extension, qua extension, simply on being applied to another extension automatically divides it – or rather, both extensions are divided by each other – then a line that is applied to another line and a surface applied to another surface would behave similarly (for they too are

15

20

25

30

559,1

---

and I have translated 'to be applied to' throughout.

[6] He means that an actually existing length or breadth is always the length or breadth of a particular body, although the concept of length or breadth is abstracted from body. The three-dimensional extension that constitutes place, on the other hand, is not a property of body, although in fact it is always occupied by body, according to Philoponus.

[7] Reading *auto* with the MSS, instead of Vitelli's *hauto*.

5   extensions); but if no such thing happens in these cases, then
    extension, qua extension, is not a cause of division. And so
    depth applied to depth would not be a cause of division, since
    it would be irrational if, of three kinds of extension, length,
    breadth and depth, length and breadth when applied to each
    other do not divide each other, but depth applied to depth does
    so.

10   So it is not extension simply, whatever kind of extension it
    may be, that is a cause of division, but extension with matter
    – that is, body. For matter is the cause of action and being
    acted on to the forms, those that are of such a nature as to act
    and be acted on at all. For not even the opposites will be acted
    on by each other if the cause of acting and being acted on is
    not in matter. (I am speaking of the natural, bodily
15 affections.)[8] So if the extension that forms place, being
    extended in three dimensions, is bodiless and matterless, it
    will not produce any effect in the body that occupies it, nor
    will any effect be produced in it by the body, since only things
    that have the same matter produce effects on each other. So
    even if the void passes through the body, there is no necessity
    that it divides it or is divided by it.

        I assert the following, too. If place, being extended in three
20 dimensions, were a body, even then there would be no
    necessity that this absurd result – I mean, that the bodies
    passing through each other be divided ad infinitum – should
    follow when the body occupying it passed through it or it
    passed through that body; but it *would* follow either that body
    passes through body, which is manifestly impossible, or else
    that one of the bodies is wholly void, so that the remaining
25 body can thus pass through it. Even Aristotle himself, after
    all, in talking of body passing through body never said it
    would follow, absurdly, that the bodies are divided ad
    infinitum in actuality, but that the greatest could be in the
    least.[9] We should recall what Aristotle himself said to those

    [8] e.g. heat and cold, when they are properties of a body, act and react so as to
    produce lukewarm. But the concept of heat does not act on the concept of cold. See also
    Corollary on Void, 688,9-25.
    [9] Aristotle *Physics* 4.6, 213b7-12. It is part of Aristotle's statement of the case made
    by proponents of the void. Void is necessary if motion is to exist, they argue, since the
    full cannot receive anything into itself: if it could, it would be possible to pack the
    largest body into the smallest, bit by bit.

who suppose growth to happen through certain voids or pores.[10] They claim that growth happens through the entrance of food into the voids contained in bodies; he objects, 30 very finely, that it will follow from this supposition either that the body is entirely void, if it grows as a whole through its 560,1 whole extension, or else that there is no growth but only a filling up of the voids. He never claimed that the void will pass through the food and divide it ad infinitum.

So this is what would be said by those who claim that place is an extension: that the body passing through the void fills it, 5 and neither is the void divided by the body occupying it, but only filled by it, nor does it divide the body. For it does not become the occupant of the body, but the body becomes the occupant of it. The void is wholly immovable, since it is bodiless. For if it were a body, it would be necessary, since the occupant of the place passes through it, that the place, being a 10 body, passes through the occupant. But since place is an extension that in its own definition is void, it will only be filled by the body that comes to occupy it. If someone is still obstinate and insists that the void passes through the body that comes to occupy it, we shall just agree with him; but even so, plainly, nothing out of the way follows for our argument, as has already been shown, since it will pass through the body without itself being moved: it is the body that comes to occupy 15 it.

It has been sufficiently demonstrated, then, that the first of Aristotle's objections has no necessary force and no plausibility or cogency at all.

(b) Aristotle's Second Objection
(*Physics* 4.4, 211b23-5)[11]

The next objection has a certain plausibility, baffling refutation by its denseness, but it too is not altogether true.

First, the reduction to the absurdity that two extensions or 20 more will be in the same place – I am not sure I would say this

---

[10] Aristotle *Physics* 4.7, 214b5-9.

[11] The second objection is extracted by Philoponus from the lines following immediately on the first objection: 'At the same time, the place too will be undergoing change; so that there will be another place which is the place of the place, and many places will be coincident.'

is an absurdity. If extension meant the same as body, then since it really is impossible for two bodies to be in the same place it would also be impossible for two extensions to be so; but in fact they do not mean the same. For first, if it is possible for two lines to be applied to each other, and not only two but
25   tens of thousands, and surfaces similarly, and lines and surfaces are nevertheless extensions and magnitudes, what prevents a three-dimensional extension from being applied to another three-dimensional one – void, I mean, being applied to body? Just as lines and surfaces, being bodiless, are thus applied to each other although they are in bodies, so what prevents place also, being bodiless, from being applied to
30   body? For in the same body in the same manner you can find plural qualities: for example, in honey, sweet, yellow, sticky, heavy, moist. So just as in these cases nothing prevents many bodiless things being in the same body in the same manner, so
561,1 also, if extension is bodiless, nothing will prevent several bodiless extensions coming to be in one and the same body, since to the one, bodiless boundary of the body it is possible to apply the boundary of another body.
5   It has now been shown well enough that nothing absurd would follow even if it should happen, place being extended in three dimensions, that multiple extensions, being bodiless, should exist in one place. For what is extended in three dimensions is not automatically a body; we shall not accept that this is a definition of body, since it is by virtue of being
10   something else that body is extended in three dimensions. Body is a substance; quantity is a property of substance, so three-dimensionality is a property of substance. But body is a substance, and hence three-dimensionality is a property of body. For it is body in that it is composed of matter and such-and-such a form, but because quantity is an inseparable property of body, therefore it is extended in three dimensions.
15   He himself said this clearly in his criticism of Melissus, and I will quote one passage from what he wrote there in support of my claim (though I could quote more) – as follows:[12] 'Melissus says that what *is* is infinite. So what *is* is a quantity, since the infinite resides in quantity, and one cannot make a substance

---

[12] The quotation is from *Physics* 1.2, 185a32-b3.

or quality or affection infinite, except accidentally in case they are quantities also at the same time. For the definition of infinite employs the term "quantity", but not "substance" or "quality".' In these words, then, Aristotle says clearly that quantity is a property of substance, and three-dimensionality 20 is a kind of quantity, and therefore three-dimensionality is a property of substance. But body is a substance; so three-dimensionality is a property of body. Now if three-dimensionality is a property of body, then three-dimensionality is not the definition of body, but is an inseparable[13] property. Hence, if something has three dimensions, it is not necessarily a body.

There is a difficulty in our argument, that we may be 25 making quantity separable from substance; but we shall look at that later, so as not to interrupt the continuity of our argument.[14] It has been shown that there is nothing impossible or absurd in the existence of multiple extensions in 562,1 the same place. And there is no necessity for those who suppose that place is an extension either to say that more than two extensions come to be in the same place, or that place comes to be in place, or that place moves at all. For the jar that moves does not move the internal extension that receives the water along with it, but rather the whole thing 5 changes its whole place. For the void is immovable. So, if you have a solid ball, and it is set in place, it will fill just so much place as its own size; and if you move it, you would not move along with it any of the void that received it, not even that which the depth of the ball filled, but the ball would fill now this, now that portion of the extension as it moved – the 10 extension remaining motionless (for how could the void be moved?). Just so, plainly, even if what is in place is not continuous but in contact, as is the case with the jar, the same will happen. For what difference does it make to apply the argument to something continuous or something in contact? There is no void unfilled by body even in that which is in contact. Just as in the case of the continuous and solid ball 15

---

[13] Reading *akhôriston*, with MS G; the others have *khôriston*, which is retained by Vitelli. See David Sedley, in *Philoponus and the Rejection of Aristotelian Science*, Richard Sorabji (ed.), London & Ithaca N.Y. 1987, 149, n. 27.
[14] See below, 578,5ff.

there remains inside it, as it is moved, no portion of the void which was occupied by parts in the depth of the ball,[15] so if you will think of it as divided so that the outside is the container and the inside the contained (for thus it would resemble the jar), when it is moved it will retain no more [of the void] than before; but, just as then it left behind as it moved the whole of the extension in which it was, and filled another in which it came to be, the extension remaining unmoved, so even if it is divided the same will happen again. For just because it is divided the ball would not fill its place in a different manner from that in which it filled it before. For its being divided has not made its place-extension move: rather, the places of its parts have become different, since the parts also have been divided in actuality. But just because the part has come to be in its own place, it does not follow that it must bring its place along with it: when the whole is moved, each of the parts leaves the part of the void which it occupied and comes to be in another.

It is not necessary, then, either that place is moved or that place comes to be in place or that a plurality of extensions are in the same [place]. For when a thing moves, it always leaves behind the former extension of place, in which it was, and comes to be in another place-extension, since the body is always in place. So only body-extension can come to be in place-extension, so that two extensions are applied to each other, the body-extension and that of the place in which the body is; but there is no third extension in the same [place], since two bodies cannot occupy the same place. For just as there can be multiple surfaces in the same [place], but it is impossible that more than two surfaces be applied to each other in actuality – namely, that of the containing body and that of the contained (for it is impossible for three bodies to be in contact with each other at the same [surface]), so I claim that even if it is possible for multiple bodiless extensions to be applied to the same one, nevertheless in actuality this never happens, because neither can two bodies be in the same place, nor void in void. For the void is immovable: even if one concedes that void comes to be in void (which is not the case),

20

25

563,1

5

10

---

[15] The moving ball does not take with it any part of the m t unless void e tension that it used to occupy, part by part.

it is clear that the void would come to be in the void in the manner in which a line comes to be in a line or a surface in a 15 surface. Just as ten thousand lines, if they coincide, do not make the whole any bigger than the original line, but the whole becomes one line again (and similarly if surfaces or points come to be in the same place they do not make bigger that in which they come to be), so if void comes to be in void the whole is just as big as the original was; for whole is 20 applied to whole. Clearly I mean the same whether I say 'void' or 'place-extension extended in three dimensions'.

It is impossible, then, that void may come to be in void or place in place or that place qua place may be moved. I take my argument to have shown well enough that none of the difficulties raised by Aristotle follow from the theory that place is an extension, void by its own definition, distinct from 25 the bodies that come to be in it.

II. Philoponus' argument against Aristotle's proposition that place is the limit of the surrounding (body)

(a) That place could not be the boundary of the container might be shown as follows. If what is in place is nothing other than body, and it is not in place by virtue of anything other than its being body, but what is in the surface of the container is not in it by virtue of being body (for body is extended in three dimensions and whatever is so extended cannot be in a 30 surface as such), it follows that place is not a surface. But the boundary of the container by virtue of which it contains the contained is a surface; hence place is not the surface of the container by virtue of which it contains the contained. For the surface is extended in two dimensions and so could not receive in itself what is extended in three dimensions, by virtue of its being such. For it is not in contact with the whole, and the 564,1 surface does not receive the whole body. For how could one say that the depth of the body is in the surface? Only the boundaries of the body are in the surface.

(b) Furthermore, if place must be equal to what is in place (this is one of the things commonly agreed about place), the 5 surface could not be place; for how can there be a surface

equal to a body? If someone says, 'I say place is equal to what is in place by virtue of the place coinciding with the boundary of the contained', let him know that he is claiming place to be equal not to what is in place but to the boundary of what is in place, and in its own right that is not even in place. If the
10   statement is true that says place must be equal not to the boundary of what is in place but to the very thing that is in place, and what is in place is a body, then the place must be equal to the body; but it is impossible for a surface to be equal to a body, since neither can a line equal a surface nor a point equal a line. So it is impossible that place be a surface.

(c) Furthermore, if place must be immovable, and the surface,
15   being the boundary of a body, is moved along with the body whose boundary it is, then it is impossible for the surface to be place. If someone says, 'Qua place it is immovable, even though qua surface it is moved', I answer that this is not true either. For it is a place by virtue of having such and such a relation to the body inside it – namely, being in contact with it and containing it; all the same, even in this respect it is not
20   immovable. For if I stand still and do not move around, the place that contains me – I mean the surface of the air by virtue of which it is in contact with me – does not remain the same but moves as the air moves, and now one, now another part of the air contains me. Similarly, if you mention the edge of the heaven nearest to us: even this is not immovable, nor does the same part of the interior surface of the heaven always touch the
25   same part of the inner body even if the things contained stand still, because all of the heaven moves in a circle. So if nothing is immovable except the earth, it is impossible that place be immovable, even if the contained be immovable. Hence, if according to common conception, as Aristotle himself says,
30   place must be immovable, and the boundary of the container is not immovable (for it moves along with that whose boundary it is, even while the contained stays immovable), it follows that place is not the boundary of the container.

565,1   (d) Furthermore, if every change [*kinêsis*][16] is either by way of

[16] The word *kinêsis* and some of its cognate forms may refer to processes of different kinds, as here, or specifically to locomotion.

alteration, or growth or diminution, or place (Aristotle himself showed that motion occurs only in these three categories, quantity, quality, and the category 'where?'),[17] which latter he calls 'locomotion' [*phora*]; and if this is divided into circular 5 and straight, – a distinction he often makes – or into locomotion and rotation, as he seems to say in the present passage; and if the outermost sphere moves in a circle, then it moves in place. For what [other] kind of change could it have? But then, what kind of place could the sphere of the fixed stars have, since there is nothing outside that contains it? Thus because the account of place given by Aristotle is not right, 10 and yet every body is in place, his account does not go through for all bodies. Hence, when they try to explain how the sphere of fixed stars could move in place when it is not in place, they throw everything into confusion rather than say anything clear and persuasive. For they cannot deny that the sphere moves in place, because they cannot even make up a story 15 about what [other] kind of motion it would have. However, they cannot explain what is the place in respect of which it moves, but like people playing dice they throw out first one account, then another, and through them all they destroy their original assumptions and agreements. For by concealing the weakness of his account with obscurity Aristotle licensed 20 those who want to to change their stories however they wish.

So some exponents say the place of the sphere of the fixed stars is the convex surface of the sphere of Cronus [Saturn], openly abolishing all the commonly agreed assumptions about place, posited by Aristotle himself, that place is outside that which is in place and contains it, and that place is equal to 25 that which is in place. For in what respect could they claim in this case that place is equal to what is in place? Moreover, it follows from saying this that the same thing in the same respect is both place and in place; for if the sphere of Cronus in respect of its convex surface is the place of the sphere of 566,1 fixed stars, but again in respect of that same surface, which is contained by the fixed sphere, is in that as in place, it follows that the same thing, namely the sphere of Cronus, in the same respect, namely its convex surface, both is the place of the

[17] *Physics* 5.2, 226a24.

fixed sphere and also is in that as in place. And how could the same thing both be the place of something and have as its place that very thing whose place it is? How can the same thing take on opposite relations with respect to the same
5 thing? It is impossible for the same man to be both father and son of the same man, if the right conception of the relation in question is preserved. In this way, then, those who say the sphere of fixed stars is in place in this manner abolish the common conceptions about place.

So, some say that the sphere of fixed stars is in place in this way,[18] others that its continuous parts are the place for each other (for each of them is contained by the parts around it);
10 and these latter again abolish the agreed assumptions. For Aristotle himself often said that the parts of a continuous body are not in place in their own right, but only coincidentally, because the whole is in place. Moreover, how must the place be no part of the thing, if its parts are place for each other? For if the whole is just what it is said to be as
15 something *of* these parts, and each of the parts contributes to the whole, then the parts are something *of* each other, since they contribute to the very being of each other, if each of them, sundered from the whole, is also going to be put out of its being.[19] Moreover, if each of the parts of the sphere of fixed stars has as its place the parts containing it round about, what kind of places are changed by the parts when they move? For they do not depart from the containing parts round about
20 them; for the heaven is not divided when it moves. How can we say that in their motion the parts yield their proper places in turn to each other? For if its containing parts are the place of each of the parts of the fixed sphere, and when the whole sphere moves it is correctly said that the parts yield their proper places to each other in turn, it must be that the heaven
25 is divided and different parts take up different positions with respect to the whole and to themselves – and that is impossible, the heaven being indivisible. For the northern

---

[18] Reading *houtô* for *autôn*, with the Laurentian MS, G.

[19] Philoponus' argument is that the parts cannot qualify as the place of each other, because qua parts of a whole they are inseparable from each other in essence. If some of them were allowed to have existence separate from others, as they must be if they are to qualify as *place* for those others, then they would no longer have existence as parts of the whole.

part never comes to be in the south or anywhere else, since
that does not happen even to things generated and
destructible, except in the case of air and water and meltable
things composed of these, such as gold, lead, wax, and so on.
So it is impossible to accept that the heaven is in place in   30
respect of its parts after this fashion.

Besides, Aristotle has just shown by means of many
considerations[20] that 'in place' is different from 'in a whole'.
But if the containing parts round about are the place of the
parts, then the part would also be in the whole as being in
place.

So the heaven is not in place in any respect. Then how does
the fixed sphere move, if it is not in place with respect either   567,1
to the whole of itself or to its parts? For what is not in place
cannot move in place. Hence, if the fixed sphere moves in
place, it is also in place. But if it is in place and is not
contained by anything outside, then place is not the boundary
of the container in respect to which it contains the contained.
The cause of this confusion is the definition of place as the   5
boundary of the container in respect to which it contains the
contained.

(e) Furthermore, it is clear from the following also that place
is not a surface. When something moves in a straight line
through a body such as air, we say that as the motion occurs   10
the air exchanges with the moving body part by part, yielding
up its place to it in turn. For body does not pass through body.
Now, if the place is the boundary of the container and is not
some different extension between the boundaries over and
above the bodies that come to be in it, then clearly during my
motion from Athens to Thebes the parts of air that yield up
their own place to me (for motion is a change of places and a   15
continuous exchange) yield up nothing but surfaces. But when
surfaces alone are put together, even an infinite number of
them, coinciding with each other they make the whole no
bigger. So how can the moving body move forwards? If they
said that along with the surfaces an extension in three
dimensions was yielded by the air to the moving body, as it   20

[20] See 4.4, 211a23ff.

progressed from one extension to another, then the result would be that it moved a distance of some magnitude – say, a stade. But if what is yielded is only a surface, and surfaces when put together make no magnitude with depth, how is it possible for the moving body to progress forwards? But it does
25   progress, and it moves whatever distance it may be – say, from Athens to Thebes: hence it is not surfaces only that are yielded to the moving body by the body that exchanges with it. But it is by exchanging its own place that it yields to the body with which it exchanges: hence place is not a surface.

III. Philoponus' defence of the claim that place is a three-dimensional extension

(a) One can see well enough from these considerations that
30   place is not the boundary of the container. That it is a certain extension in three dimensions, different from the bodies that come to be in it, bodiless in its own definition – dimensions alone,[21] empty of body (for void and place are in reality the same in substance[22]) – this may be shown by elimination of the alternatives. For if place is neither matter nor form nor the boundary of the container, it remains that it is the extension.[23]

568,1   But it can also be shown directly by itself that there is a certain extension of this kind, altogether different from the bodies that come to be in it; and first, from what has just been described, namely the exchange of bodies. For how do we say bodies exchange with each other? If the moving thing does not
5   pass through body, and further the moving thing is not a surface but extended in three dimensions, then when it has cut through the air and come to be in its place, obviously the air exchanges with it just as much in quantity as the moving thing is itself. Now since the measure is just as large as what is measured, it follows necessarily that if the air is ten solid

---

[21] English translation cannot retain cognate words for *diastêma*, an extension, and *diastaseis*, its dimensions.

[22] 'Substance' here translates *hupokeimenon*. Philoponus does not mean to imply that void or place are substances (*ousiai*) in the technical sense of being structures in which form and matter can be distinguished, but that they differ only in their accidental properties.

[23] See Translator's Note above (p. 14).

cubits the space that received is the same quantity. So it also   10
is ten solid cubits, and that is obviously what is yielded up to
the moving thing, which is just as large as itself. But that was
the place: it is places that they exchange with each other.
Hence place is something solid, meaning by 'solid' extended in
three dimensions.

But place also is a measure of things in place, and therefore
is equal to them. This can be shown more clearly by the case of   15
the jar. Suppose there were no extension inside the hollow
surface of the jar filled at the time with air, having the same
solid measure as the air that is in it, but rather it is only a
surface that received the air: then since the jar is a measure
and the measure must necessarily be equal to what is
measured, it is reasonable to conclude that it received only the
surface of the air too, and that is absurd. For when the air   20
exchanges with the water, the water that takes the place of
the air is solid and a body. So if the water is measured by the
jar, and the measure is as large in quantity as what is
measured by it, since the water is solid and not a surface the
measure also must be solid. Certainly, when we have filled the
jar and measured the water, we say that the space in the jar is   25
as large as the water is. Did we then measure the surface of
the water, to see how big its perimeter is? No, we measured
the solid. Therefore we do not make any claim about what
kind of shape the measure has; we look only at the solid
contents. So when we say that the *space* in the jar is as large
as the solid measure of the water, do we mean that the *air*
that was in the jar before the water was so large? Not at all;   569,1
for it is not the case that the water passed through the air and
was measured by the air: the air got out of the way of the
water. But do we mean that the surface of the jar is so large?
Not at all; for our purpose in all this was not to measure
planes, but solids. It remains, then, that we measure the   5
space between the boundaries of the jar. The extension in
between *is* something, then, over and above the bodies that
come to be in it.

Of course, I do not mean that this extension either ever is or
can be empty of all body. Not at all. But I do claim that it is
something different, over and above the bodies that come to be
in it, and empty by its own definition, although never without   10

body; in just the same way we claim that matter is different from the forms, but can never be without form. In this way, then, we conceive the extension to be different from all body and empty in its own definition, but various bodies are always coming to be in it, now this one, now that, while it remains unmoved both as a whole and in its parts – as a whole,

15 because the cosmic extension which receives the body of the whole cosmos can never move, and in its parts, because it is impossible for an extension that is bodiless and empty in its own definition to move.

(b) Furthermore, to one who looks to the truth the *force* of the void will clearly establish both points – I mean, both that the

20 extension is something over and above the bodies that come to be in it, and that this is never without body.[24] What about clepsydras – I mean the things popularly called 'snatchers' here among our people?[25] The vessel is filled with water; there are many perforations in the base: when we stop the hole in

[24] The concept of 'the force of the void' is the origin of the medieval *horror vacui*, on which see Edward Grant, *Much Ado About Nothing*, Cambridge 1981, 67-100.

It is not clear where exactly the phrase originated. It occurs in the essay *de Febribus* attributed to Alexander of Aphrodisias (7,2), also in Philoponus *de Aeternitate Mundi contra Aristotelem*, quoted by Simplicius, *de Caelo* 158,17 (see now the translation in this series by Christian Wildberg, London 1987, 93-5).

An earlier version of the concept is 'following on to what is being emptied' (*pros to kenoumenon akolouthia*), which is a phrase used by the physician Erasistratus (third century BC), probably borrowed from the Peripatetic Strato. See my note in Furley and Wilkie, *Galen on Respiration and the Arteries,* Princeton 1984, 32-7.

[25] The clepsydra (literally 'stealer of liquid') was a hollow vessel, sealed over at the top except for a narrow vent or bent tube which could be plugged with the thumb; the bottom was perforated to form a strainer. It was used domestically for transferring liquids from one vessel to another without moving the vessels. The clepsydra was lowered into the liquid with the top vent open, until it was filled through the pores of the strainer at the bottom. Then the vent was plugged, and the clepsydra lifted out, retaining the liquid, and transferred to the second vessel. Then the liquid was released by unplugging the top vent.

I was once told that clepsydras could be bought in rural markets in (I think) Wisconsin, but I have never found one. There is a drawing in W.K.C. Guthrie, *Aristotle on the Heavens*, Loeb Classical Library, 228.

Clepsydras became a standard model for demonstrating the unseen physical powers of air from the time of Empedocles (fifth century BC), who used it in his theory of respiration. Aristotle quotes the relevant lines of his poem, in *de Respiratione* 7 (Empedocles fr. 100). My article 'Empedocles and the clepsydra' (in Allen and Furley, *Studies in Presocratic Philosophy* vol. 2, London 1975, 265-74) offers an interpretation; for another, see M.R. Wright, *Empedocles: The Extant Fragments*, Yale 1981, 244-8.

The fact that air *always* takes the place of what is 'emptied' out of a vessel was taken by Aristotle as a disproof of the existence of void. See *Physics* 4.4, 211b18-19, and Simplicius *in Phys.* 573,2-27.

its mouth with a finger, the water will not go out through the perforations in the base in spite of being heavy and having so 25 many exits, but rests supported on the air at the perforations, held aloft contrary to nature. But when we unblock the upper hole, the water goes out through the perforations in the base with some force. The cause of this is nothing but the force of the void; for since there cannot be a void, when the upper exit is blocked, if the water were to go out from underneath, the air 30 will not be able to move around from anywhere into the interior to replace the water as it leaves – neither from above, because the upper mouth is totally blocked by the finger, nor from below, because since the perforations are very tiny and the water is pressing on them the air is not strong enough to 570,1 force a way through the water to find an entrance, and water cannot exit and air enter at the same time. So the water tends to move downward and the air pushes back, and because of the natural force of the void in the whole system there is deadlock. If the holes were bigger, with more water in them, 5 the air in one part could be overcome and yield to the water; then as the natural impulse of the water went in the direction where the air in one part yielded, the air in the other part, as the force of the water shifted to the first, would then be able to get an entrance. This happens also with perforated jars when they are full: since the wine does not flow out with force, but 10 because of the pressure of the air flows only gently down through the pot, they therefore bore holes up above in the empty regions where there is no wine, so that having given entrance to the air up there they make the exit of the wine unhindered. At least, it can be seen to flow with force then.

How does it happen that water, which by nature tends to move downward, is moved upwards by those who drop a pipe 15 into it and suck upwards through it? By sucking out the air in the pipe you create the risk of a void forming in the middle, and so the famous force of the void moves the water contrary to nature. At least, in this way they empty whole pots. They make half of the pipe bend backwards, lower one end of it into the pot, then suck the air out of it through the other end, and 20 so draw the water out with it by the force of the void, and the water having once begun to move does not stop until the whole jar is emptied.

This happens for the following reason. When the water hurries to fill the whole pipe, reaches the bend, and begins to
25 move with its natural motion, the air is not strong enough to push it back in the reverse direction, because of the natural impulse of the water and the crooked shape of the pipe at the bend. So, since the air cannot enter and it is impossible for the pipe to become empty, the flow of the water into the pipe becomes continuous. For if, as the water right at the beginning entered the pipe and reached as far as the bend in
571,1 the pipe, no other water entered from below, and if the air was unable to force a way past the water and fill up that part of the pipe, then necessarily it would become empty. So the force of the void, always filling up what is being emptied, does not cease until the water in the jar is exhausted and the pipe is filled with air from below from the end – I mean the end that
5 is sealed into the jar. For the jar, obviously, is filled with air through its mouth as the water exits through the pipe; and this air that comes to be in the jar after the water is exhausted exits continuously along with the last of the water entering [the pipe], and so fills up the bottom parts of the pipe in which there is no water.

Now, if there were, in the middle of the clepsydra or the
10 aforesaid pipe, no extension distinct from the body in it, void in its own definition, how in the world does nature either prevent the water in the case of the clepsydra from moving according to nature when the upper mouth is blocked, or in the case of these pipes make it move upwards against nature? The common riposte everyone gives is 'so that there may not
15 be a void'. And what void was ever likely to occur, my dear sir, if there is no distinct extension between the boundaries of the jar over and above the extension of the water? Then when the water left, nothing would remain but the concave surface of the jar. So what was it that was likely to become void? The surface? But no one in his right mind, I suppose, will call a
20 surface either full or empty. For if a surface, qua surface, is of such a nature as to be filled with some body, how much is the air – I mean, in volume – that fills the surface of the earth? You cannot determine it. How much is that which fills the surface of this cube, let us say? An inch, or more, or less? And what is there surprising about that? For that it is not possible

to determine <it> can be seen from the fact that you can put
another body closer to or further away from the cube, without,   25
of course, being able to call the surface of the cube either fuller
or emptier at these various distances.[26]

This, too, makes it clear that the surface cannot be either
full or empty. It is agreed that there cannot be a void, and that
there cannot be anything outside the convex surface of the
sphere of fixed stars; and clearly, again, no one in his right   572,1
mind will say that the exterior surface is either empty or full.
Now, if place is a surface, and there is no extension that is
empty by its own definition, what power is it in nature that
often moves bodies in the direction contrary to nature, so that
a void may not occur, if there is in the universe no extension   5
that is at risk of becoming void?

(c) Surely they cannot claim that void means the failure of the
surface to be in contact with a body, on the ground that there
is an absolute natural necessity that every body is in contact
with something? That would be to introduce the thesis that
every bounded thing is bounded against something, which
Aristotle proved well enough to be false;[27] for being bounded   10
and being in contact are different, and the latter is relative,
the former not. And it has been shown too that there is
nothing outside the heaven; so the heaven is not in contact
with anything. And in any case, if the universe is not infinite,
its exterior must necessarily be in contact with nothing. But
even if the interior parts of a body are in all cases in contact
with something, all the same that is an accidental property of   15
them, he says; so if being in contact is an accidental property
of them, even if they are not in contact their nature is not
thereby infringed. But that this is not what void is – I mean,
the failure of body to be in contact with body – is clear from
the following: if it were this, then how does Aristotle show
that there is no void outside the heaven? If he says the surface   20
is void when it is contact with no body, what is outside the
heaven is obviously void also, since the outside surface of the

---

[26] I am not sure that I understand this. Is Philoponus' point that to fill something
must be a matter of degree, but the only relevant activity admitting a more and a less
is to approach another body, getting more or less close to its surface – and that
manifestly has nothing to do with filling it?

[27] *Physics* 3.8, 208a11ff.

heaven is not in contact with anything. But he says that there is no void outside the heaven: so void is not the failure to be in contact with anything.[28]

Again, if void is not being in contact with a body, it is clear that Aristotle, in his discussion of the void, investigates this

25   proposition – namely, that every body must necessarily be in contact with some body. But that is absurd: for how could he say that there is no void, not only within the cosmos, but also outside the the cosmos? According to his own view the heaven is in contact with no body on the outside. Why should I say more? I shall set down the words of the philosopher [sc. Aristotle] himself, revealing both what everyone takes the void to be, and that he himself shows this void to be

30   non-existent. 'Those who claim there is void,' he says,[29] 'posit it as a kind of place or vessel; it is thought to be full when it contains the mass that it is capable of receiving, void when it

573,1   is without it.' And again:[30] 'People mean by void an extension in which there is no perceptible body.' And he himself, inquiring what the conception of void signifies, says that in one way void is called an extended space not full of perceptible body, and in another that in which there is no 'this' nor any

5   bodily substance; so from this definition matter, too, is called void.[31] And in saying that these two things are meant by the word 'void', he did not say that 'void' means a body not being in contact with any other body at its surface; even when he objects to the existence of void, he shows that it does not exist in the sense of what the word itself actually means and what

10   everybody understands by it – namely, a three-dimensional extension having no body in it. Hence the same arguments, he says,[32] that have proved that place is not an extension, will also prove that void does not exist, since place so described and void are the same thing.

So if void does not mean what is in contact with nothing, but is an extension in which there is no body, and if there is in the

15   middle of the snatcher and the pipe we discussed no extension distinct from the bodies that come to be in it, then it is surely

28 See Aristotle *de Caelo* 1.9, 279a12ff.
29 *Physics* 4.6, 213a15-18.
30 ibid. 213a26-9.
31 *Physics* 4.7, 214a6-12.
32 ibid. 214a16.

plain that even if the water departs void is not left behind; for there is no distinct extension. So why does nature force the water, against nature, to stay where it is or move? Clearly, so that the interior may not remain empty, presuming that there *is* an extension in the middle of the boundaries, which was filled with water – a space which, if the water departs and air 20 does not replace it, risks being empty.

(d) I think, then, it has been clearly shown by these arguments that there is an extension distinct from the bodies that come to be in it, empty according to its own proper definition, and this is also place, in the strict sense. But consider the following, too. If bodies that come into being do not require outside themselves 25 an extension equal to themselves in three dimensions, why in the world do wineskins and jars break through the agency of the grape-juice when the wine changes to pneuma? If God, in creating bodies, did not append to them an extension that yields to their substance, but just introduced those substances themselves without need for a place distinct from them, why is it not the case that the body that comes to be in the wineskin 574,1 needs nothing to yield to it?[33] For it is an accident of bodies that body is in contact with body, since the universe is not continuous but divided. Thus according to Aristotle one [sc. body] is the place of another, but it does not come to be in order to be the place of that (for the heaven did not come to be in order 5 to be the place of the bodies inside it): it is an accident arising from the order of the things that come to be and their natural tendencies to motion that one is the place of another. Now, if being in contact with each other is an accident of bodies, and in their being they have no need of an extension outside themselves that will receive them, it would have to be the case, as I said, that the body that came to be in the wineskin when the grape-juice fermented would need no other place outside itself. 10 But in fact it does; at any rate, it bursts the wineskins, because in its own nature it cannot be without extension, nor can the same extension of space receive two bodies.

[33] Philoponus introduces the Christian concept of a Creator and a simple teleology, but they are not in fact essential to the argument. The argument aims to show that it is an *essential* property of bodies that they need an extended space to be in, whereas Aristotle's conception of place makes the relation between body and place an *accidental* one.

(e) Consider the following. If there is no distinct extension receiving them, over and above the bodies that come to be in it, let us in thought remove the bodies in the middle and see if
15   it is really so. So then, if we think of the bodies within the heaven as not being there – I mean earth, water, air, and fire – what would remain in the middle but an empty extension? For it was plainly possible to extend straight lines from the centre to the circumference everywhere: so what is it through which we draw the lines but empty extension extended in
20   three dimensions? Let no one say that the hypothesis is impossible. (It was not a conclusion from my argument; when a hypothesis has an impossible consequence, from the impossibility of the consequence we refute the hypothesis.)[34] For we often make impossible hypotheses for the sake of seeing the nature of things in themselves. Aristotle himself,
25   objecting to those who claim that the earth stands unmoved because of the rapid rotation of the heaven, says 'If we stop the heaven in theory, where will it [sc. the earth] move to.'[35] And again in turn, he studies bodies in and of themselves by separating them from all quality and all form; and we arrive
575,1   at a conception of matter by separating all form from it and studying it naked, all by itself. It is not absurd to use hypotheses even if they are impossible, for examination of other things; on this ground, since some people explained the stationary position of the earth by the motion of the heaven, Aristotle says that we should stop the heaven in theory, and
5   ask where the earth will go by nature, so as to see whether the movement of the heaven really is the cause of the stationary position of the earth. Plato, too, separating in thought the cause of the order of the universe from the cosmos, asks how the universe would be, all by itself and without God. Each of these cannot possibly come about; all the same, theory
10   separates in thought things naturally conjoined, so as to see how each thing is by itself in its own nature. And so I too, since some will not admit that what receives bodies is an extension distinct from them, but maintain that the only thing extended in three dimensions in the nature of things

[34] I have changed Vitelli's punctuation here. The connective *epeitoi ge* in line 23 seems to be linked to 'Let no one say the hypothesis is impossible.'
[35] *de Caelo* 295a21ff. The quotation is not exact.

that exist is body-extension – I too in the same way say: if it is
so, grant me in theory that the bodies inside the heaven are 15
not there. So, is no empty extension left in the middle? But I
think it is obvious: for if there were nothing between the
boundaries of the concave surface of the heaven, the
boundaries of the heaven would collapse when the interior
bodies were removed in thought. But that is impossible, since
it is not because of the interior bodies that the heaven is as it
is: it would still be the same, if there were nothing there.[36] 20

(f) What we saw in the case of the whole cosmos can also be
seen in the case of the part. Let us suppose there is a bronze
sphere, not full but half empty. It is of course obvious that
what was trapped inside was air. Now if I think of the interior
air, not indeed destroyed into non-being but changing to earth
or water (this of course being not impossible), since the earth 25
or water that has come into being obviously takes up a smaller
place than the air, the remainder, in which there was
formerly air but now there is nothing, is necessarily empty.
But Themistius says,[37] objecting to this, that the bronze of the
hollow sphere will collapse sooner than the body inside flows
out or changes into earth. And what he says is true,
unwittingly. For why, tell me, did the bronze collapse? Surely 30
it was not kept up by the body inside it, as wineskins are by
the air when they are blown up? So what is the reason for the
bronze collapsing? Is it anything but the fact that the
extension in the middle does not stay empty? But, even
though nature does not allow this, let it be granted me, in 576,1
theory, that the bronze does not collapse and the air inside
does change to earth, and you will see that there is an
extension in the middle distinct from the bodies in it. What is
absurd in this, that just as we separate matter in theory from
all forms for the purpose of studying its nature, even though it
is impossible that this should ever happen, so we also suppose 5
hypothetically that the air trapped in the middle of the bronze

[36] This is a strange argument. The collapse of the heavens is of course as
theoretical as the removal of the interior bodies. Why should the heavens not collapse
in theory? It must be because their nature as a set of hollow spheres is essential to
them, and not conceptually dependent on the fact that the hollow interior is filled.
Philoponus would no doubt defend this by claiming that God made them so.
[37] Themistius *Paraphrasis* 114,7-12

sphere changes to earth without the sphere collapsing, so that we may observe the consequence? But what I postulate is not outside nature, but happens daily – I mean, the change of a little air into earth. What in general is the necessity for the
10 bronze to collapse when the air inside changes to earth? For if there is no extension inside, distinct from the contained body, what is the danger that the bronze will necessarily collapse when the air changes?

Themistius[38] was wrong to object to Galen: the latter postulated hypothetically that no other body flowed in when the water in the jar was removed, in order to study the
15 consequence, and he objected that he was begging the question. He says: 'But let us suppose that no other body flowed in when the water was removed, so there remains a separate extension inside the surface [sc. the inner surface of the walls of the jar]. But the hypothesis is irrational, my wise and clever Galen: it hypothesises the very thing we are inquiring about. We inquire whether there can be a separated
20 extension – and you say "let us suppose there is a separated extension." So you invent your own extension and draw it just as you want, but you don't demonstrate what is really there.'

So says Themistius; but I believe it is obvious to everyone that his answer is silly. If it was agreed that the extension exists, but one asked whether it can exist by itself, empty of body, as Aristotle does ask in the following passage,[39] and
25 then Galen hypothesised that when the water flows out no other body enters instead, he was indeed begging the question. But since that is not the question now, but whether there is any extension at all, distinct from body-extension, which is the place of bodies, and Galen claims that when the water has departed no other body enters, he does not say, as
30 you claim, Themistius, 'Let there be an extension separate from the bodies inside the jar,' but 'Let no other body enter when the water runs out, and so let us see whether there is
577,1 anything inside or not.' If in general you think that when the

---

[38] Themistius, ibid. Simplicius (*in Phys.* 573,16-25) sets out the same argument as Philoponus, in much the same words, but without mentioning Themistius. He gives the sentence 'But let us suppose that no other body flowed in when the water was removed, so there remains a separate extension inside the surface' as a quotation from Galen, but it cannot be found in the extant works of Galen.
[39] *Physics* 4.7, 214b16ff.

water has run out, if we do not hypothesise another body entering, it follows that there is a separated extension inside, you yourself are caught on your own wings: for you say there is another extension inside, but it is never empty of body, as we too agree. For we do not say that this extension ever 5 remains empty of body, but that it is different from all the bodies that come to be in it although it never comes to be empty of body; and for this reason there is interchange of bodies and the force of the void, so that place-extension may never remain empty of body.

(g) It must be understood that the hypothesis put up by 10 Themistius, on the ground that some say place-extension is like body-extension without qualities, is altogether far from the truth. For that extension is nothing but quality-less body. So for those who say this the expected consequence will be other absurdities and especially that body passes through body. But we do not say that. For we do not say that the 15 extension is body, but that it is space for body, and dimensions alone, empty and apart from all substance and matter.[40] Such a place has all the commonly agreed properties of place. For it is just as much equal to what is in the place as the boundary of the container is, and it is immovable, as he [sc. Aristotle] said, and it is no part of the thing, and separable, and it too encompasses what is in the place just as much as the 20 boundary of the container does.[41] For just as those who say the surface is place say that it contains, although it is applied to the boundary of the body, so also the extension, even if it is applied to the body, would contain it, because void is not what comes to be in the body, but body is what comes to be in the void, as I already said.

For if place were a body-extension and a body came to be in 25 it, then the extensions would necessarily pass through each other; but since in itself place is void, it would not be reasonable to say that it passes through the body, but that the body passes through it. When the body comes to be in it, what

[40] See above, 567,32

[41] i.e. it satisfies these requirements, set out in Aristotle's *Physics* 4.4, just as well as Aristotle's definition does. I do not understand why Philoponus says *ouden mallon* rather than *ouden hêtton*.

happens is only filling, not passing through each other. For
this reason also the part will not in itself be in place; for if the
578,1   body that passed inside the place were actually divided by the
extension, it would necessarily follow that because each part
is individually outlined each part is individually in place; but
if the body is not divided by the extension and the extension
does not pass through the body, why should it necessarily
follow that the part is in place in itself?

5   (h) But the following difficulty might be raised against the
argument – a difficulty we have already mentioned in
advance:[42] if place is an extension without any substance or
matter, having its being in its dimensions alone, and
dimensions belong to [the category of] quantity, it will follow
that quantity can exist in separation from substance. But that
is impossible, since all the other categories have their being in
10   substance. So if it is impossible that quantity subsist by itself
in separation from substance, it is impossible for such an
extension to exist. Now I say that what is above all necessary
is not for the nature of the facts to follow along with our
theories, but for our agreed ideas to be consistent with the
facts. So because we have determined that it is impossible for
a quantity to subsist without substance, it does not follow at
15   once by necessity that the nature of the facts is like that. For if
it is from the fact that we always see quantity in bodies
together with substance that we demonstrate that it could not
subsist by itself, then it is time to remark that substances
themselves are not self-subsistent.[43] For every natural
substance requires some determinate quantity for its being. It
is impossible that any form can subsist in any random
20   magnitude, as was shown in the first book of this treatise:[44]

[42] See 561,25ff.
[43] *authupostatos*: literally 'self-hypostatised', translated also as 'self-constituted'.
The concept of self-subsistence is central to the Neoplatonic theory of ontology and
causation, particularly of Proclus (see *Elements of Theology*, propositions 40-51). It
refers to entities capable of existing actually by themselves without the need of
another being as substrate. They are self-generated, perpetual (not temporal),
non-composite, imperishable, and therefore immaterial. See further J. Whittaker,
'The historical background of Proclus' doctrine of the *authupostata*', in *De Jamblique
à Proclus*, Fondation Hardt, Entretiens 21, 1974, 193-230. I am indebted to an
anonymous reader for this note.
[44] *Physics* 1.4, 187b13ff.

flesh, man, bone, and all other natural forms could not subsist except in a determinate quantity, and if the quantity that is natural for the subsistence of flesh is destroyed, the form is destroyed along with it. Thus I would say that natural forms have their being in quantity as in a substrate. And what is one to say about quantity? None of the natural forms could subsist 25 without matter; so all are properties accidental to matter.

To understand the truth about these matters would require a long discussion and a lot of time; but as I said at the beginning and say now, let them either show that there is no such extension and destroy our demonstrations, or, so long as the latter still hold up, we shall not do away with the nature of the 30 facts just because some people thought they had shown that quantity cannot subsist by itself.

Furthermore it is also possible to assert that none of the categories subsist without implicating each other; for it is not 579,1 possible to discover one category subsisting without implication with the others, not even substance itself which is said to be able to subsist by itself. Matter, too, and the second substrate – I mean body that is extended in three dimensions and without quality – though in its own right it can subsist by 5 itself, nevertheless does not ever subsist without qualities. So place-extension, too, even if in its own right it could subsist by itself (for what could prevent space from being empty of body, as we said,[45] if we think of the jar containing no body inside it?), does not, all the same, ever remain empty of body all by itself. Just as, in the case of matter, when form is destroyed, another 10 form at once takes over, so too in this case the exchange of bodies never leaves the space empty: simultaneously one body departs, and another rushes in instead. And thus it is never possible to find even this kind of quantity without substance. Perhaps this is what 'the force of the void' is – that this kind of quantity is never in separation from substance.

Thus, then, we can also save what seems to have been agreed 15 upon through our habit of continually saying it: I mean, that quantity cannot subsist without substance. For the void can never exist in separation from body.

---

[45] 568,14ff.

(i) But we have not yet shown that place under this description has all the properties that belong to place: I am
20 referring to the distinction between up and down in place taken as a whole. For the following objection might reasonably be raised by someone on behalf of the Aristotelian view: If the three-dimensional void enclosed within the concave surface of the lunar sphere is the place of heavy and light bodies, as you yourselves maintain, and if light bodies
25 move by nature to the upper place and heavy bodies to the lowermost place, how will you determine what is up and what is down in this extension? For at what point will you define one direction as up and the other as down? And if place must have some natural power by virtue of which light and heavy bodies, seeking their proper places, each move to their own
580,1 region by natural impulse, but the extension you describe, being void in its own definition, cannot have any power, then what is the reason why some things have a natural impulse to move to one part of it and others to the opposite part? If, then, what must above all things belong to place is up and down, and that distinction cannot be a property of your kind of place
5 but only of that boundary of the container in respect of which it contains its contents (which was Aristotle's definition of place), then the latter must be place in the proper sense.

For since things that are better and upper stand in the relation of form to things that are more deficient, which obviously occupy the position of matter to them, and since matter desires form, as female desires male and the base
10 desires the noble (for each desires being, and each has being just when it attains its proper perfection, which is its form), it is therefore reasonable that fire desires its own natural place, that is, to be contained by the surface of the lunar sphere, so that it may be ordered and as it were formed by it. It is ordered and perfected by it by virtue of the one acting and the other's being acted on, and the action and being acted on occur
15 only by contact. In the same way, air desires to be contained by the sphere of fire, and so on to the end.

But the answer to this is easy: Aristotle's account is just as much liable to the same objections. For if place is the boundary of the container, and the contents are contained by
20 different surfaces of air or water, according to the largeness or

smallness of each, let the Aristotelians tell us up to what point we are to determine the place that is down. There are mountains that because of their enormous size almost touch on the lunar sphere (hence they are called 'Moon-Mountains'):[46] if we imagine them not continuous with the earth but divided from it, in which place will they be said to be, up or down? And what am I to say about this? The rocks lying on the top of the these mountains, or parts of earth or of water, separated from the whole mass, that are around the centre of the cosmos – are they in the place that is down? Then the air that is below those mountains must be in an unnatural place, since it is lower than the heavy bodies. Even if the higher parts of the mountains are not imagined as being separate, but as being continuous with the whole earth, as indeed they are, are we to say that the surface of the air that contains their peaks is a part of the place that is down or not? And how far are we to carry this? And we shall say the same about the place that is up. For what will you say it is? The concave surface of the lunar sphere? But if only this is the place that is up, and only the things that are proximately contained by this are in the place that is up, then air is not in the place that is up, since it is proximately contained, not by this sphere, but by that of fire. If this too is up, then there are two kinds of place that are up. And the same story holds with respect to down, regarding earth and water. And what will the difference be between the place that is up and itself, and similarly with down?[47]

Hence it is clear that the same problems follow no less from this account also; but what the truth is can be learnt from the following. Properly speaking, there can be no up and down by nature in the cosmos; as he [sc. Aristotle] says elsewhere,[48]

25

30

581,1

5

[46] Moon-Mountains are mentioned in Ptolemy's *Geography* and elsewhere. The ancients saw the Mountains of the Moon as the source of the Nile. The mountain range may be that of Kilimanjaro. Others identify them with the Ruwenzori mountain range in East Central Africa on the Uganda-Zaire border. They were discovered by Henry Stanley in 1889. They peak to about 5,120 m and are covered with extensive glaciers. Covered in mist they present a strange and awesome sight. I am indebted to an anonymous reader for this note.

[47] i.e. if there are two kinds of place that are up, how is up to be distinguished from itself? How are the two kinds to be distinguished? Is one of them down with respect to the other? Can up be down? Can down be up?

[48] See *de Caelo* 4.1, 308a17ff.

10   there can only be the circular and the circumference. If we call
the circumference 'up' and the middle 'down', the place
occupied by heavy bodies will be down, and that occupied by
light bodies will be up. For things standing on the tops of
mountains are overtopping the whole by force. I say 'by force'
because even if they are continuous with the whole earth, they
are not in continuous contact with it everywhere; they are like

15   stones laid one on top of another in buildings. The
unnaturalness of their position is shown up well enough when
they break off. In that case, being unnaturally situated, they
move to their proper and natural place. It is quite ridiculous
to say that place has any power in its own right: it is not
through desire for a surface that things move each to its

20   proper place, but through desire for that station in the order
which they have been given by the Creator. Now since earth
received the last station, so as to be underneath everything,
and water the second, and air and fire the third and fourth, it
is understandable that, when this order is somehow disturbed
and a thing whose nature is to float on another is somehow
forced not to float but to sink under it, through desire for the

25   station in order given them by the Creator they move just so
far until they have achieved this. Hence light things move
upwards, desiring not simply to be in contact with the surface
of the container, but rather desiring the station which the
Creator allotted to them. For then they have their being most
fully, and then they achieve their perfection. So it is not place

30   that has the power to move bodies to their proper places; it is
the bodies that have a desire to keep their own station.

The elements, then, are four, two of them light, two heavy;
if I must give a general definition, I assert that that part of the
extension which receives light bodies is up, and that part

582,1 which receives heavy ones is down. But Aristotle cannot say
which is the place that is properly speaking up and which is
down. For if the place that is up belongs to light bodies and
down belongs to heavy, and the place that is up is the
boundary of the container, and this is the concave surface of

5   the lunar sphere, and this is the proximate container only of
fire, then either air will not be up, or there will be two kinds of
the place that is up. And similarly with down. And if he wants
the spheres inside the sphere of the fixed stars also to be in

place, and in place there is in all cases up and down, then one
will be up and another down, one heavy and another light –
and he does not want that. So we must not in all cases divide 10
place into up and down, even on his own suppositions. Why
cannot the same thing be both container and contained? For
the sea, if it is in place, must be contained by the surface that
supports it, which is obviously the earth, along with the air
that is on top of it. But similarly, if the whole earth is in place
in respect to the whole of itself, it must be contained with
respect to a part of itself by the surface of the water at the 15
bottom of the sea. Hence, the surface of the earth is the place
of water, and that of the water is the place of the earth, and
the same thing contains in the same respect as it is contained.
None of these difficulties follow for those who say place is the
extension.

(j) But they raise another objection against our account. They
say that if there really is such an extension, void by its own 20
definition and capable of receiving bodies, it must be infinite.
For it will not have any boundary, since a boundary is a
surface of things extended in three dimensions – and what
surface could such an extension have, since surface exists
[only] in bodies? Hence, if the whole bodiliness of the heaven
is stretched through it right up to the outermost surface, and
there cannot be a limit of it, it must be extended outside the 25
heaven to infinity; and this is irrational just in itself, as well
as having been sufficiently refuted by Aristotle both in this
treatise and in *de Caelo*.[49]
But I do not know how such an objection can even be
thought to be plausible. For first, just as one may imagine
such a three-dimensional extension, so one may imagine a
surface analogous to it; secondly, even if one could not 30
imagine a surface analogous to it, still the void would not
necessarily be extended to infinity for this reason. For since it
subsists as the place of bodies, so much of it subsists as can
be occupied by the bodies of the cosmos, but it is coterminous
with the boundaries of these bodies. If the interior of a jar be
imagined as empty, and different bodies are placed in the jar, 583,1

[49] *Physics* 3.4, 204a1ff. *De Caelo* 1.9, 278b20ff.

not continuous with each other but in contact, so that each occupies a part of the place inside, then each of these parts of the void must be coterminous with the body received by it, and
5   the whole of the void, right up to the concave surface of the jar, must be bounded, as all the bodies inside it right up to that surface are bounded. Just so, in the universe each of the spheres inside it occupies a bounded part of the void, and the whole is coterminous with the whole of the cosmos, having a boundary that is not only its own: for it is not impossible to imagine that this, too, has a surface, as there is in all cases a
10   boundary of the occupying part of the interior bodies, and to imagine the surface of the outermost body coinciding, as I said, with the boundary of the void.

(k) However, when we made these points against what Aristotle said about place, a defence was put forward by the
15   Philosopher.[50] Being a philosopher of nature, Aristotle discusses those things which exist and are organised by nature, and nature is a principle of motion and rest:[51] so if that is what nature is, whatever things are natural have in themselves a principle of motion and rest. So whatever things do not have in themselves a principle of motion and rest are
20   not natural; and so the philosopher of nature will not discuss them. Now extension of the kind we describe, having no principle of motion and rest in itself (for it does not grow or change or move in place, and does not even come into being nor perish), cannot be a natural thing. Since Aristotle's discourse is concerned with natural things, he now inquires
25   what is the place of natural things, being obviously a natural philosopher himself. It is understandable, then, that he denies that an extension such as we describe is the place of natural bodies, whether it exists or not (for it is not natural), and that the only natural place for bodies that he finds among natural things is the boundary of the container with which it contains the contents.

[50] This is presumably Ammonius. Philoponus often calls Aristotle 'the Philosopher', and in *de Aeternitate Mundi* he often refers to Proclus by this title without naming him. But he refers to 'the philosopher Ammonius' in his commentary on *de Anima* 473,10, and Ammonius is the obvious 'Philosopher' with whom Philoponus engaged in conversation. See Sorabji, in *Philoponus and the Rejection of Aristotelian Science*, 3-4.
[51] See *Physics* 2.1.

My reply to this is as follows. If in fact Aristotle never 30
discussed whether such an extension exists or not, but only
sought to show that the place of natural bodies is not such an
extension (i.e. three-dimensional), then perhaps there would
be some plausibility in the Philosopher's reasoning, showing
that Aristotle was not denying the existence of such an
extension, but only its claim to be the place of natural bodies,
being a natural thing itself. But since Aristotle explicitly and 584,1
continually, both here and in his discussion of the void,
attempts to show that there *is* no extension other than
body-extensions, the Philosopher's defence of Aristotle is
shown to be fictitious. Again, to say that because such an
extension is immovable it is not recognised by the natural 5
philosopher, because the natural philosopher discusses
natural things, and natural things are things that have a
principle of motion and rest – this too is plainly contrary to
Aristotle's view; for he clearly wants place to be immovable
with respect to every kind of change. Here are his own words:
'So when the thing inside moves and changes in something
that is moved, like a boat in a river, it treats the container as a 10
vessel rather than as place. Place is meant to be immovable;
so it is rather the whole river that is the place, because as a
whole it is immovable. Hence this is what place is: the first
immovable boundary of the container.'[52] And a little before
this, attempting to show that place is not extension, he
reduced the argument to the absurd consequence that the 15
place itself must change: so he means its unchangeability to
be an axiomatic property of place. And that is understandable; for if place, qua place, changes, it must change either in
substance or in quantity or in quality or in place. But it cannot
change in substance, since it is not a substance, nor in quality,
since place is a quantity rather than a quality, and still less 20
can it change in place, since there will then be another place of
the place. And that it does not change in quantity either, by
increase or diminution, is testified by Aristotle himself. For he
puts this among the difficulties concerning place, that one of
the agreed features is that increase and diminution are not
among its properties.[53] But if he means place to be 25

[52] *Physics* 4.4, 212a15-21.
[53] *Physics* 4.1, 209a26-30.

unchangeable, then he would not reject the extension as the place of natural bodies because of its unchangeability: he attempted to do away with it for this reason, that he believed that such an extension as we describe does not exist at all. Moreover, many natural things, discussed by the natural philosopher, are immovable: e.g. the centres of the spheres, or the poles. Souls, too, are immovable with any natural motion, in Aristotle's view above all – not only rational souls but irrational too, and they are plainly natural kinds of life: all the same, the natural philosopher discusses them. Hence, if Aristotle had believed in its existence at all, he would not have attempted to show that such an extension as is the subject of our discussion did not exist at all because of its being immovable.

John Philoponus: Corollary on Void

Commentary on Aristotle's *Physics* pp. 675-95

I. Philoponus' criticism of Aristotle's arguments against the existence of void extension

At this point, then, the arguments about the void are complete for Aristotle. But we must return to an earlier point in the discussion and examine each of the arguments. We shall begin not from the beginning of his own discussion of the void *675,15* (for we have already stated our own opposition to some of the arguments in their own place), but from where he began to argue that if there is a void there can be no motion through it, as there is in fact through air or water.[1] Of all his arguments these are the most beautiful, and they have snared nearly everyone by their persuasiveness: I mean those drawn from the unequal speed of moving things.

Before beginning the discussion I repeat what I said in my *20* discussion of place,[2] namely that our discussion does not seek to establish that there is a void existing in its own right and separate and without body, and that motion takes place through it. Not at all. I agree that there is no void separate altogether from body; I am persuaded by the so-called 'force' of *25* the void and many other things.[3] My objection is against the arguments of Aristotle aiming to show that if there were a void nothing would move through it, and <my contention is> that even if there is no void separate altogether from bodies there is nevertheless the void that is filled, which is also the

[1] i.e. Not from *Physics* 4.6 but from 4.8. He draws on the *Corollary on Place* for objections to some passages before 4.8: for example 624,26ff., 632,4ff.
[2] *Corollary on Place* 567,30ff.
[3] See the *Corollary on Place* 569,18, with note ad loc.

49

676,1   place of bodies, as we showed earlier. And now we shall show
that the arguments against this position are not cogent, even
if they are seductively plausible. But first we must recall the
arguments summarily.

(a) Summary of Aristotle's arguments

A. *Physics* 4.8, 215a24-b22

Of the unequal motion of bodies there are two causes: first, a
5   difference in the medium through which they move, even
though the moving bodies are equal and alike, and second, a
difference in the moving bodies, even though the medium
through which they move is one and the same. So he takes
first the same moving body and supposes this to move first
through water and then through air, taking equal distances of
each, and he finds that it moves through the water in a longer
10   time than through the air. He assumes that as one time is to
the other, so water is to air in its consistency; for as the time
though the water exceeds that through air, so water is thicker
and harder to part than air. Now, since there is this
proportional relation between the times, the motions, and the
15   media through which they move (for if there is motion
through void, he says, it will of course take time), then the
time of motion through the void will have a certain
proportional relation to that through the full. But this is
impossible, since what is *nothing* can be in no proportion to
what *is*. Hence neither will the times of the motions have any
20   proportional relation to each other. But every finite time is in
proportion to every finite time: hence it will move through the
void in *no* time, and that is to say it will not move, since there
is no motion without time.

B. *Physics* 4.8, 215b22-216a4

The second argument is clear. If there is motion through void,
it will turn out that the same distance is traversed through
25   void and full; and this is absurd. For if I take a body finer than
air in the same proportion to air that the time for void bears to
the time for air, and insert this body in the extension of the

void, then it will move through this very thin body in as much time as it took to move through the void. So in the same time it will move an equal distance whether full or void, which is impossible.

C. *Physics* 4.8, 216a11-21

These, then, are the arguments that he draws from a 30
difference in the media through which motion takes place.
But if we take the medium to be the same, and the moving
bodies to be different, we shall find again, he says, that it is
impossible for motion to occur in a void. When two unequal or
dissimilar bodies, he says, move in the same medium in
unequal times, we can state the reason: namely, that the
heavier, because it parts the medium more quickly, descends 677,1
in less time; and similarly in the case of bodies of equal mass[4]
but different shape, that which parts more air (that is, the
broad one) descends more slowly, and that which parts less,
more rapidly, since less air is parted more rapidly than more.
But if the motion is through a void, since what is parted is 5
nothing, all will move at equal speed.[5] For why should one
move faster, another slower? But it is impossible that all
things should move at equal speed: hence it is impossible for
motion to happen in a void.

(b) Criticism of these arguments

Argument C

These, then, are the arguments by which he denies the
existence of void on the basis of motion. Let us first examine 10
the last one – I mean whether, if we posit a void, everything
that moves through it must necessarily move at equal speed,
from which the denial of motion through a void is derived. To
begin with, it must be objected to this, that he demolishes his
own theses by the very means he uses to establish this. For if

[4] The word *onkos*, here translated 'mass', is an imprecise, non-technical word, usually meaning bulk or massiveness, although it is sometimes used to denote three-dimensional space (not in Euclid's *Elements*).

[5] Contrast Epicurus, *Letter to Herodotus* 61: 'All atoms must move at equal speed, when they travel through the void without collision.'

a difference in motions occurs not only from a difference in the
15 media through which motion takes place but also from a
difference in the moving bodies themselves, if one is heavier
that the other, then plainly there is a cause of unequal motion
in the moving bodies, over and above the difference in motion
that occurs from the difference in the media through which
they move. But if this is so, then clearly even if they move
20 through a void their motion must be different, since the
moving cause that is in them is different. If we have two
unequal masses – say, a ton and a pound – and if in their
motion in a void there is no difference with respect to faster
and slower, but unequal bodies have the same speed of motion
through one and the same nature, viz. the void, then if we fill
25 this void through which our unequally heavy bodies move
with equal speed with an airy body, it is to be expected that
they will move with equal speed through this air. For the
nature of air by its introduction has not added anything to
their substance and made one of them more inclined to fall
and the other less. It has done nothing to their substance, nor
introduced any greater impulse in either of them. But it is
impossible that unequal bodies move with equal speed in the
30 same medium.

If they were to get more contentious and say 'Yes, unequal
bodies moving through void *will* move at the same speed, but
through a bodily medium with unequal speed', then plainly
the supposed body through which the motion takes place is
the only cause of the unequal motion, since there is no
678,1 difference to be attributed to the moving bodies themselves.
For whatever by its elimination also eliminates the difference
between faster and slower must be the only cause of that
difference. So the medium will be the only cause of the
unequal motion. But as well as demolishing Aristotle's own
5 theses, this is refuted as being plainly false. For if this were
the only cause of the unequal motion, bodies unequal in
respect of their impulses must have moved with equal speed
through one and the same bodily medium, if no difference is to
be attributed to their different impulses, and unequal motions
must come about only when the media are different – and this
is contrary to the evidence. For it is evident that unequal
bodies, moving through the same medium, move with unequal

speed – because, of course, the moving causes in them are   10
different, and being different they must by their own agency
produce activities that are different also, even if they are
moving their underlying bodies not through a bodily medium
but through a void.[6]

Furthermore, he himself, having declared that there are
two causes of unequal motion, a difference in the medium and
a difference in the moving body, goes on to say *how* the   15
medium is a cause of different motion. 'The medium through
which motion takes place,' he says (215a29), 'is a cause,
because it impedes the motion by contrary motion and by
remaining unmoved,' since it needs to be parted. Now if there
are two causes of the fact that bodies do not all move at equal
speed, the difference of the media and the difference of the
moving bodies, and the cause to be attributed to the medium
is an obstructing cause, then the cause to be attributed to the   20
difference in the moving bodies must be an active cause; for
one could not conceive of any other. If, then, the obstruction is
removed, there remains none the less that cause of unequal
motion that is in the moving bodies – the active cause. For of
course weight does not have its being in the state of something
else: it is a quality in its own right belonging to bodies. So
since weight is the active cause of the motion downward, as he   25
too believes,[7] when there is an extension for the body to move
through – I mean, void – and when the active cause of the
motion is different, and there is nothing to obstruct the
motion, motion even through the void must inevitably be
unequal. Hence, even if there were a void, unequal motion
would not be done away with.

Furthermore, unless unequal bodies, in their own right,
have the cause of unequal motion, even if they move not
through a bodily medium but through a void, why is it that   679,1
when a ton weight and a pound weight move through air, the
ton falls faster? For if the air is homogeneous and the bodies
in their own right are equally fast, what is the cause of their

---

[6] By 'substrate bodies' he means simply the bodies to which these impulses belong
as properties.

[7] The following passage, from 678,24-684,10, appears (with some omissions) translated by Morris R. Cohen and I.E. Drabkin in *A Source Book in Greek Science*, Cambridge, MA 1966, 217-21, under the heading 'Anti-Aristotelian views on the laws of
falling bodies'.

unequal motion? The air, being one and the same, should be
5 the cause of the same effects. So it is clear that the impulses of
the bodies, one of them being naturally more inclined to fall
and the other less so, contain in that fact the difference in the
unequal motion. For the one with a greater downward
tendency parts <the medium> better. For what other reason
can we give for the air being parted faster by the heavier, than
10 that the one that has a greater heavy impulse has more
downward tendency by its own nature, even if it is not moving
through a bodily medium? Having more downward tendency,
it pushes the air aside more effectively by the force of its
onrush, and the air, being pushed more effectively, gets out of
the way faster. Hence, if it cuts more by having more
downward tendency, even if what it cuts is nothing it will
none the less have more downward tendency. For what has
15 greater impulse does not have more downward tendency
because it cuts more: it cuts more because it has more
downward tendency. Moving does not follow from cutting, but
cutting from moving, when motion takes place through a
bodily medium. But if bodies in themselves have more or less
downward tendency, they will obviously have such a
difference among themselves even if they move in a void and
20 the same distance in a void will be traversed in less time by
the heavier and in more by the lighter, not because of being
more or less obstructed, but because of having a greater or
lesser downward tendency in proportion to the difference in
their natural weight.

For qualities are not relative, and do not have their being in
a relation to each other, like vision and the visible. Colour, as
25 a visible, is a relative, but as white colour or dark colour it is
something else and not relative. Its being colour does not
belong to it because of something else, but because of itself;
colour is a quality. So weight and lightness do not belong to
the things that have them because of something other than
themselves, and weight is an active cause of downward
30 motion, and lightness of upward motion, whenever things
that have weight or lightness are in the place that is contrary
to their nature and there is nothing obstructing their motion.

For the clod of earth held up or hung up in air, although it is
in the place that is unnatural to it, nevertheless does not move

downward, because of what obstructs it. And in water too a piece of wood does not naturally move and go downward but floats on the water, because of its being finer in the 680,1 distribution of its parts, and having much actual air distributed in it; so since air does not naturally sink in water but rises to its surface, consequently the wood does not sink through the water but is held up by its large content of air, as happens with inflated bags. So in these cases, too, that which 5 impedes the motion, the air, being more forceful, prevents the natural downward motion of the wood in water. Wood does fall, however, in air. This is because each thing, when in the whole mass of its own <kind>, does not naturally become active with respect to its own natural impulse; so since the air in the wood is not active in air with respect to its natural impulse, the natural weight of the wood moves the wood 10 downwards because it is in the place that is not natural to it. And that this air, distributed in actuality in the wood, being not inclined to sink in water, moves towards its proper whole mass, and thus makes the wood float on water (which also happens, as I mentioned, with <inflated> bags) – this is proved by the denser woods, such as boxwood and ebony. Because of the density of their substance, they have no air 15 distributed in them to give an upward thrust, and so they sink downward even in water because of their own weight, since nothing obstructs that motion.

Everywhere, then, the innate impulse moves in this way towards its own because of nothing but itself, if there is nothing to obstruct it. So if the impulses have a downward or upward tendency, not because of their relation to something 20 else, but because of themselves, when the weight of bodies is different their downward motion must be different too, from no other cause but the weight itself. For no impulse is a relative thing. And we shall say the same with regard to lightness too.

It has been shown well enough, then, that even if motion took place through a void, it would not be necessary that all things move with equal speed, and that there is no cogency in 25 the argument by which Aristotle thinks he has established this. With this shown, the first point at issue is also proved at the same time – I mean, that it is possible for motion through

void to take time. For if in general faster and slower motions
are preserved even in a void, and faster and slower are
30   distinguished by time (for what traverses a given extension in
a longer time is slow-moving, and likewise what takes a
shorter time is fast-moving), then clearly even bodies moving
in a void, if indeed the medium through which the motion took
681,1 place were void, would always take time in their motion.

Argument B

We shall now show in turn that the absurdities Aristotle
thinks he derives as following from the proposition that there
can be motion though void do not follow from it. For if bodies
have their downward tendency from no other cause than their
5   own innate impulses, and from this cause the heavier body
falls in less time,[8] even if its motion takes place through a
void; and further if the body through which things move when
they do move through a bodily medium is an obstruction to
their motion, then obviously the time taken by each motion is
proportional to the impulses inherent in the <moving>
bodies, even if there is no obstruction – I mean, no body
10   through which the motion is taking place, such as air or
water. For if the medium is a cause of unequal motion qua
obstruction, then the innate impulses must be active causes.
So even if the obstruction is removed, some time is taken by
the motion of each thing – more or less of it in proportion to
the greater or lesser impulse. But if some time is taken in the
15   motion because of each of the impulses in itself, it will never
come about that one and the same thing traverses in the same
time an equal distance in the full and in the void. For if
something traverses an extension a stade long filled with air,
and the moving thing is not at one and the same instant at the
beginning and the end of the stade, a certain time is taken
because of the moving bodies in themselves (since, as I said,
they are not at both ends at the same instant), even if the
20   extension is void, until they get from the beginning to the end;

---

[8] The text has *en pleioni khronôi*, 'in more time', but that is probably just a careless
mistake. Wolff 149n reads *mallon to* (with the MSS) for *to mallon*, and translates 'und
vor allem deswegen das Schwere eine endliche Zeit braucht'. I suppose he takes
pleioni to mean 'more than zero', but I find that impossible.

and a certain *other* time is taken because of the obstruction, since the pushing or parting of the medium makes the moving thing less mobile. So the more fine-grained we take the air through which it moves to be, the more the time taken for parting the air is diminished, and if the bodily medium is 25 thinned to infinity, the time will also be diminished to infinity (for time is infinitely divisible); but it will never, even if the bodily medium is thinned to infinity, reach that time which it took to traverse a stade through a void.[9]

I will make the argument clearer by means of examples. If the moving body were a stone, and it moved through an 30 extension of a stade, that extension being void, there will

[9] Philoponus is arguing against Aristotle *Physics* 4.8, 215a29-216a7.
Aristotle made two initial assumptions: (a) that (other things being equal) the speed of a moving body varies proportionately to the thickness or thinness of the medium through which it moves; and (b) a body moving over a distance through a void would take some time greater than zero to traverse it. Suppose a body B moves over distance D

(1) through a thick medium M^1 in a long time t^1
(2) through a thinner medium M^2 in a shorter time t^2.

Then, from assumption (a), we have

$M^1:M^2::t^1:t^2$.

But, from assumption (b), B moves over D through a void in a very short time, say t^3, shorter than t^2. But given assumption (a), there must be a very thin medium M^3, such that

$M^1:M^2:M^3::t^1:t^2:t^3$,

and B must traverse D through medium M^3 in t^3. Thus B takes the same time, t^3, to traverse distance D both through a void and through medium M^3.
Aristotle took this result to be impossible, and took that as a proof that assumption (b) is wrong. He claimed that it is wrong because there *is* no void extension.
In the present passage, Philoponus claims that it is assumption (a) that is wrong. Other things being equal, it is not the whole time taken by the movement that varies in proportion to the thickness of the medium, but only the *extra* time needed to overcome the resistance of the medium, over and above the time due to other causes. Thus in effect he rewrites Aristotle's equations as follows. Suppose body B moves over distance D taking time T due to its own nature and the distance. Then it moves

(1) through a thick medium M^1 in time $T + t^1$
(2) through a thinner medium M^2 in a shorter time $T + t^2$
(3) through a void (thickness zero) in time $T + 0$.

The extra time needed to part the medium, t^1, t^2, ... gets less and less as the medium gets thinner and thinner, but never reaches zero so long as there *is* a bodily medium. So the time taken to traverse even the thinnest medium never equals the time taken to traverse a void.

necessarily be some time that it takes in moving over the extension of a stade – say, an hour. Now if we suppose this extension of a stade to be filled with water, it will no longer

682,1 traverse the stade in one hour; an extra time will be added because of the obstruction. So let another one hour be taken for parting the water. So the same weight has moved in an hour through void, in two hours through water. Now, if you thin the water and make it into air, if air is twice as thin as

5 water, the time spent in parting the water will be lessened proportionately. That was one hour. So it will move over the same extension through air in one and a half hours. And if you again make the air twice as thin, it will move in one and a quarter hours. And if you thin the bodily medium to infinity, you will lessen to infinity the time taken for parting the bodily

10 medium – I mean the one hour – but you will never exhaust it. For time is divisible to infinity. But if you never exhaust the time by thinning the bodily medium, but always when motion is through a bodily medium some part of that extra hour is added in proportion to the thinness of the medium, it is

15 obvious that it will never traverse a stade in the same time through a void and through a plenum. It moved through a void in one hour, through a bodily medium in one hour and a bit. However much you suppose the medium to be thinned, the hour is never exhausted. Hence it will never traverse the same extension, full and void, in equal time.

Aristotle reached that conclusion [sc. that it will traverse the same extension, full and void, in equal time] by doing

20 away with his own assumptions – I mean, that differing motions depend also on the difference in the moving bodies. For if there is a certain time that differs according to the different impulses, and there is another time caused by the parting of the bodily medium through which the motion takes place, the same extension will never be traversed in equal

25 time both full and void. For suppose we say: 'If it moves a stade through a bodily medium in two hours, and through a void in one, if I take a body that is so much thinner – say, twice as thin – then it will move the same extension in half of the time, namely one hour, through the thinner bodily medium. But it moved the same extension also through a

void.'[10] But this is totally false, and contrary to to the obvious. For it untruly supposes that whatever proportion the bodily media bear to each other is also the proportion the times of motion bear to each other, and vice versa. That, indeed, appears to be plausible and its refutation is hard to find at once, because of our inability to grasp what proportion air bears to water in respect of consistency: i.e. by what measure water is thicker than air or this piece of air than another. But it is possible to refute it from the moving bodies themselves. For if, as the times of the motions are to each other, so must the bodily media of the motions be to each other, given that one and the same body is moving through both, since the motions vary not only with the medium but also with the moving body, then it is reasonable to suppose that if the bodily medium of the motion were one and the same but the moving bodies were different in respect of their impulses, then as the impulses are to each other, so are the times of the motions to each other. For example, if the impulse is double, the time is half, and if a two pound weight falls a stade through air in an hour, a one pound weight will fall over the same extension in half an hour. And, vice versa, as the times are to each other, so must the moving bodies be to each other. But that is entirely false. And one can prove it from the plain facts better than by demonstrative argument.

For if you take two weights differing from each other by a very wide measure, and drop them from the same height, you will see that the ratio of the times of their motion does not correspond with the ratio of their weights, but the difference between the times is much less. Thus if the weights did not differ by a wide measure, but if one were, say, double, and the other half, the times will not differ at all from each other, or, if they do, it will be by an imperceptible amount, although the weights did not have that kind of difference between them, but differed in the ratio of two to one. But if, when the moving bodies are different but the bodily medium is one and the same, the two moving bodies do *not* have the same proportion to each other that the times of motion have to each other, nor the times the same as the bodies, it stands to reason, then,

30

683,1

5

10

15

20

25

---

[10] Vitelli marks a lacuna here – unnecessarily, I think.

30   that also when the moving bodies are the same and alike but
the media through which they move are different (like air and
water), the times of motion through air and water do *not* have
the same proportion to each other as air has to water, nor do
the air and water through which the motion takes place have
the same proportion as the times. But if the difference in the
times does not follow in proportion with the difference in the
bodily media, then supposing the bodily medium is twice as

684,1 thin, the motion will not take half of the time, but more than
half; and as I said before, as one thins the bodily medium, so
one lessens the time that is added from the parting of the
bodily medium, but one never exhausts it or lessens it in
proportion to the thinning, as I said. For the body will not

5   move through a medium that is twice as thin in half the time.
Hence, if the time is not reduced by the same measure as the
medium is thinned, but by thinning the medium we reduce
but never exhaust the time that is added[11] from parting the
bodily medium through which the motion occurs, then a thing
will never move over the same extension full and void in equal
time.

Argument A

10   Along with this proof it will also have been proved that the
void will never have any proportion to the full; nor does that
follow from the proposition that motion can take place
through a void. Now, it is clear that the void will never have
the *same* proportion as the full,[12] since the times cannot be
the same, i.e. the time taken through the void and that

15   through the full, given that the extensions are equal; and it
has been said that, given that the times have some proportion
to each other, it does not necessarily follow that the media
through which the motion takes place have *that* proportion to
each other. But that the void cannot have any proportion
whatever to the full, even if the times of the motions have
some proportion to each other, is clear from the following.

20   For if (a) the difference in the motions varies not only with

---

[11] Reading *prostithemenos* in 684,9, for the MS reading *prostithemenou*.
[12] i.e. The proportion between distance and time will never be the same through a void and through a plenum.

the media but also with the moving bodies themselves, and (b)
the medium is a cause of the time by impeding the motion,
and (c) it impedes by virtue of the consistency of its bodiliness,
which requires time to be parted, and (d) when the motion
takes place through a void time is consumed, since the body
cannot be at both ends at once, but the time is of this or that 25
length according to the proper impulse of each body, and (e)
because of the void itself, qua void, moving bodies take no
time, as they do because of the bodily medium when they
move through a bodily medium (because the void has no
consistency at all, such as some kind of bodiliness, so as to
require parting, but exists for the moving thing just as a
bodiless extension and a space [*khôra*], offering it no 30
obstruction at all): how then can it be said that if there were
motion through a void the void would have some proportion to
the full in respect of consistency?

For if some time is taken in the motion because of the bodily
consistency and the density of the medium, whereas no time
at all is taken because of the void as such, then since there are
no times to be compared to each other – I mean, the time
through void and that through a bodily medium – but just one 685,1
time, neither can the void be compared with or have any
proportion to the full. For if it was from the times' having a
proportional relation to each other that Aristotle deduced that
the void, too, has a proportional relation to the full, then since
it has been shown that some time is added, when things move 5
through a bodily medium, because of the bodily medium as
such, but no time at all is added, when things move through
void, because of the void as such, it follows necessarily that,
since the times of the void and the bodily medium have no
proportional relation to each other, because there *are* no two
times at all, but only the one due to the bodily medium,
neither do void and body have any proportional relation to
each other. Simply as extensions – say, cubits or stades – the 10
void and the full have a proportion to each other by virtue just
of their bodiless magnitudes and their quantity (for the times
taken by things moving through them, qua extensions of such
and such size, also have a proportional relation with each
other); but if one is filled with body and the other is void, it is
no longer necessary that the full one has a proportional 15

relation with the void one in respect of its consistency and
density and bodiliness, since the times belonging to these
items themselves, as such, are not comparable to each other,
as I said, but time is added in the motion because of the bodily
20   medium, whereas no time at all is added because of the void
as such. Hence, since the time added because of the bodily
medium has no proportional relation to some other time
added because of some consistency of the void, neither does
the void as such have any proportional relation to the body as
such.

The error in reasoning occurred because he wanted to
transfer the proportional relation of the times, however they
are taken, without any qualification or exception, to what the
25   time is predicated of. For since we say that the time of motion
through air is, say, double the time of motion through a void,
it follows, he says, that air has the same proportional relation
to void in respect of its bodily consistency, and is as it were
twice as thick. But this assumption is wrong. In that way I
30   might argue that since a certain time has elapsed while I
think of this theorem – say, one hour – and one hour is the
time that belongs to such thinking, and two hours have
elapsed during the motion of a stone a certain distance
through water, it follows that since the times have a
proportional relation to each other the things of which the
time is predicated must have that same relation to each other.
686,1   Let there be, then, a two-to-one relation in consistency
between water and thought, the movement and the thinking,
the stone and the theorem; but that is ridiculous. Yet their
times have a proportional relation to each other; even so, no
one would be crazy enough to say that these things will have a
proportional relation to each other, whether the same or any
other.
5   And what shall I say about changes[13] of different kinds? If
one thing is heated for one hour, and another blackened for
two hours, or if both are blackened, one for one hour and one
for two, it does not follow that the changing things are to each
other in consistency as the times are to each other. Again,
from the fact that the time of the moon's motion has some

---

[13] The word *kineisthai* and its cognates may of course denote changes other than
change in place, as here.

proportional relation to the time of the motion of Mercury, it 10
does not follow either that their spheres have the same relation
to each other in consistency, or that the places in which they
move do. Again, from the fact that the time of every rectilinear
motion through a bodily medium has a proportional relation to
the time of the motion of the lunar sphere, it does not follow
that the places where they move, namely air and the surface 15
that surrounds the moon, have the same proportional relation
to each other, or that they are commensurable at all; for things
different in kind are not commensurable, as Aristotle himself
remarked.[14] In all cases, then, it has become clear that, if
certain times have a proportional relation to each other, it does
not follow immediately that the things to which the times
belong have some proportional relation to each other. For time
has one and the same nature that measures every motion, but 20
not every motion is commensurable with every other, nor is
every medium through which motion takes place commensurable with every other. For qualitative change is not commensurable to growth, nor change in knowledge to whitening or
blackening. So just as in these cases the times have a
proportional relation to each other, but what the times are
predicated of are incomparable because they are of different 25
kinds, so I claim about the case before us that the time through
the void has a proportional relation to the time through the
bodily medium, because every time has a determinate proportional relation to every time, but the void has no proportional
relation to the full, since they are of different kinds from each
other.

Criticism of argument in *Physics* 4.8, 216a26-b21

Our discussion has now sufficiently examined the arguments 30
from motion in place; there remains an argument that the void
does not fill the need of bodies for a *place*, from which it follows
that it is useless – or rather, that it does not even exist, since
there is nothing useless among the things that have come to
be.[15] If the void exists, he says, it follows that a body placed in it

---

[14] *Metaph.* 10.4, 1055a6. *ta men gar diapheronta ouk ekhei hodon eis allêla, all'
apekhei pleon kai asumblêta.*

[15] Philoponus now turns to the next section of Aristotle's *Physics*, 4.8,

occupies an extension of the void as great as itself. So, he says,
since the body is in place in no other respect than as being an
extension, if we detach from it everything that has nothing to
do with its being in place, such as its colour, weight, and so on,
nothing will be left but its extension. So there will be no
difference between the void and that extension. But if there is
no difference between the extension of the body and that of
the void, why was it necessary to put another extension
around bodies from outside, when each body has its own
extension from inside? So bodies have no need of the void. And
if two similar extensions passed through each other, two
bodies will do so, too. For it is by virtue of nothing but their
being extensions that bodies are unable to pass through each
other. It is not by virtue of being qualified that they do not
pass through each other (for nothing prevents many qualities
coinciding), but by virtue of being extensions. But if two, why
not more? Again, if an extension qua extension needs another
extension, then the void will need another void (since the void
is an extension), and so there will be void in void.

Against this, my first reply is as follows. If we have shown
in our discussion of place that of necessity there is among the
things that exist an extension of this kind, empty of all body in
its own proper definition, which is also the place of bodies, it is
useless to claim that, if there is an extension in every body,
putting another extension around bodies from the outside is
superfluous. For we do not make up the natures of things, but
try to understand how things are, and if ever we are unable to
give the reasons why things happen, we are not obliged to
deny their existence too. So now, let them refute the
arguments by which we showed that there is such an
extension; otherwise, if our arguments are true, it is really
useless to deny what exists because of an inability to give the
reasons for its existence, or because of an inability to solve the
apparent difficulties confronting the account of it. It is like
denying the existence of an animal part because you cannot
give the reason for it. If the thing exists one must try to solve

---

216a26-216b21. It is amusing to note that Philoponus copies Aristotle in beginning
with a pun. Aristotle begins: 'It will appear that the alleged vacuum is truly vacuous'
(*to legomenon kenon hôs alêthôs kenon*). Philoponus begins: 'The void does not even
fill the need for a place' (*oude topou khreian ... plêroi to kenon*).

the difficulties confronting the account of it, not deny its nature because of them.

Secondly, he is wrong to identify the void with body. For if 30 you remove every quality from the body, even then the bodily extension is not the same as the void. For even if we take away every quality from the body, there will still remain the massed matter and the unqualified body, which is composed of matter and form in the category of quantity; but the void is not composed of matter and form. For it is not a body at all, but bodiless and matterless – space without body. So if what 35 remains when all the qualities are removed from body is nevertheless body, and the void is not a body, it will never be the case that body is in body, if the body is in the void as in 688,1 place.

But 'Yes,' he insists; 'for if the extension is in place qua extension, let its matter, too, be taken away from it. Being bodiless in its own right, that is not in place at all. So then the extension belonging to the body will be no different from the 5 void.' But one who argues thus must realise that he is asking for the impossible. For that body, which we say is in place and is unable to pass through another body, is nothing other than the compound of matter and form. So if the matter is taken away, the form of body vanishes at the same time, because it has its being in matter.

When we say that white is sight-piercing, we mean that this 10 property belongs to it not otherwise than as in a substrate, which is the body.[16] And when we say that opposites cannot co-exist in the same thing, we mean opposites that belong to substrate bodies – for example, the hot and the cold, in body. And if we imagine them without body, we shall at once have taken away from them this mode of being; for if we imagine opposites *not* in a substrate body, they will not conflict with 15 each other at all, and nothing stops them being united. For in the genus, it has been shown that nothing stops opposites from being in actuality, and one and the same soul unites their definitions, and even the knowledge of opposites is one and the same.[17] And white will not be sight-piercing unless it

---

[16] For this definition of 'white', see Plato *Timaeus* 67E, Aristotle *Topics* (passim) and *Metaph*. 1.7, 1057b8.

[17] Philoponus gives three cases in which opposites, not being in a body, can be seen

20   is in a body, nor black sight-compressing. So too, then, if you
      think of bodily extension without matter, it will no longer be
      in place,[18] since it is no longer a natural thing, and such an
      extension would not be said to be unable to pass through body.
      Indeed, it will not even be extended, except in its conceptual
      formula – or rather, there will not even be such a body in
      reality at all, unless one is speaking of the conceptual model
      (*paradeigma*) or the defining formula. But our present
25   discussion does not concern them: our inquiry is about the
      things of nature.

      Hence the body that is said to be in place must necessarily
      be none other than the physical body, that is to say, the
      compound of matter and form. When this, then, is in the void
      as in place, it will not follow that body is in body, since the
      void is not a body at all, nor is the void useless, if indeed it is a
30   place of bodies. Moreover, neither will the body qua extension
      be in another extension: rather, qua bodily extension it will be
      in place-extension. So there is no necessity that the void too be
      in another extension, if it is not qua extension that the body is
      in a place-extension, but qua body. And we showed well
      enough also in our discussion of place that it does not follow
      that body passes through body if the body is in the void as in
      place.[19]

      If you object, 'Since there is extension in everything and it
689,1 moves around with its bodies, what need is there to put
      another extension around bodies on the outside?', I reply, 'It is
      because physical bodies always exist, move, and rest *in place*.'
      For I claim that it is impossible for motion in place to occur
      without the existence of such an extension. Now, if we all
5   agree according to common conception that bodies are in
      place, and we showed previously that the place of physical
      bodies is none other than extension of the kind that we
      describe (for body is in place qua body, and body is
      three-dimensional, and so it is in place in its three

      to co-exist in some sense. (1) In a genus, the species may have opposite characteristics
      (animals may be aquatic or terrestrial). (2) A soul or mind can entertain the thought
      of a pair of opposites with regard to the same thing. (3) Even scientific knowledge (the
      point of 'even' is probably that this case is not jus   contingeht, a the others are)
      comprises opposites (geometry handles straight ar   curved lines) It is only in an
      individual body that opposites cannot co-exis . See al o *Corolla y on Place* 559,9-19.

      [18] Reading *te* at 688,21, for the MS reading *de*.

      [19] *Corollary on Place* 557,10ff.

dimensions; but in that case it is necessary that its place be
extended in three ways, in order to receive in its own three 10
dimensions that which is itself three-dimensional) – well, if it
must be the case that there is a place for physical bodies and a
common conception agrees on this, and place was shown to be
that extension, then such an extension must indeed exist. We
shall proceed to show that motion in place would not exist if
this did not exist; of course I do not mean, if void did not exist in 15
isolation, all by itself (I have often indicated this), but rather,
void that is such in its proper definition but always full of body.

To say 'if two extensions pass through each other, why not
three?' is to make a pointless objection in reality. It is not
possible for bodily extension to pass through bodily extension,
nor for void to come to be in void, since the void is motionless,
being totally non-bodily. So, if void cannot come to be in void 20
nor body in body, but only body can come to be in void as the
filler in the filled, only two extensions therefore can be
together, body-extension in place-extension; never three. For
neither can void come to be in void nor body in body, nor two
bodies in one and the same place. 25

II. Philoponus' defence of the existence of void extension

We have now said enough to show that none of the arguments
demolishing the void are cogent. We shall now show, first, that
even if there were void in isolation and deprived of all body,
that would in no way prevent motion in place from occurring
through it, and second, what I have said already, that there
could be no motion in place at all if there were not such an 30
extension, in its proper definition deprived of body, even if
never without body in it.

If there were, then, a void extension isolated from body, there
would be nothing to prevent bodies moving through it *in time*,
and moving faster and slower too: that has been shown already 690,1
by the refutation of the arguments purporting to make this
case. We must also try to show it independently.

(a) First, then, if there is circular motion, and it is not one and
the same but differentiated (for the <heavenly> spheres move
in different ways, one faster, another slower); and if the things 5

moving in circles do not move *through* some body (for they do not move by parting first one, then another bit of body, but rather circle round upon themselves without cutting any body at all, and the sphere of fixed stars does not even touch anything on the outside); if the spheres, then, without cutting through body nevertheless move *in time*, and one faster, one slower, then motion occurring through body is not the reason either for the consumption of time or for differences of speed of motion. It is because of the difference in the power that is in the moving objects that faster and slower motion occurs. As to the consumption of time in motion generally (if there is a superlatively fast motion such as that of the sphere of fixed stars), they are right to suppose that the reason is the form of motion itself: I mean that every motion is from here to there, and it is impossible for one and the same thing at one and the same instant to be in this place and in that. If, then, the fastest of all existing things, parting no body in its motion, nevertheless moves in time because of the nature of motion itself, why not also things that move in straight lines, even if they should move through a void? Because of the motion itself they move in time, and because of differences in their innate impulse they will have differences in speed. For if *they* [sc. the heavenly spheres] take time in all their motions although they part no body, and they have differences in speed for no other reason than the innate powers in them, among things that are generated and perishable too, it will obviously follow when they move through a void that they move in time and have differences of speed.

Furthermore, if we have shown in our discussion of place that in all cases every body fills an empty space, plainly the heavenly bodies have filled an empty space, in which they also move. But if the heavenly bodies, making their motion through the void (for one part of the heaven occupies one part of the void and another another), move in time and have differences of speed, all the more will things moving in straight lines, even if they move through a void, move in time and have differences of speed. For, if the whole reason for motion's taking time were the body parted in the motion, and if therefore it followed necessarily that things moving in a void move without time because there is nothing for them to part, all the more would this have to happen in the case of the fastest of all motions – namely, that of the circumference [sc. of the cosmos]. For what moves in a circle parts no body either. But it does not happen: every rotation is in time, even though there is nothing parted in the motion. All the more, 5 then, will this not happen with things moving in straight lines, but even if they were moving in a void, in all cases they would move in time and there would be nothing to prevent differences of speed.

(b) Furthermore, the argument can be refuted from the motions of choice, which belong to us as living beings. Suppose the interval between earth and heaven were void, and I 10 wanted to walk from Athens to Thebes: should I get from Athens to Thebes in no time? Absurd! For I should be simultaneously and at the very same instant in Athens and in Thebes – and indeed everywhere. Suppose I wanted to walk, say, from Athens to Italy, and this had to happen in no time because my motion was through a void, I would have to be simultaneously and at the same instant in Athens and in 15 Italy, and in that case also in all the intervening lands, and in that case everywhere, if you imagine someone walking around the perimeter of the earth.

And what if one walked faster and another slower, this motion being continuous? Would they both complete the same walk in no time together? Then what advantage did the the 20 greater walking power have over the lesser, or a runner over a weak woman? But if nothing prevents walking through a void in time, and walking is a movement in place, then nothing prevents motion through a void if there is a void. If it is universally true that the motions brought about by soul could happen even if there were a void, what prevents the natural 25 motions also from happening through a void, in time?

Suppose someone objects to my argument, using what is said at the end of the *Physics*,[20] and claims that in walking it is not only motion that is observed, but also rest, since you have to plant one foot and push the other past it. This objector would claim that time was taken in the walking, not because

---

[20] *Physics* 8.8, 262a17-21.

30   of the motion, but because of the rest. I would reply that the
rest is not of the whole body but of a part of it, but the motion
is of the whole body and is continuous and uninterrupted. The
rest is partial, because it is a property of each of the two feet in
turn. That the whole body does not stand still but moves
continuously is clear from the following. Nature caused one of
35   the feet to rest because of the motion of the whole. We move
the whole body by means of the counterthrust of one foot. It is
692,1 in this very counterthrust and resting of one foot that the
whole body is moved. For if the whole is at rest during the
counterthrust of the foot, when does it move? One of the feet is
always thrusting, since the whole body cannot levitate. So
either the whole does not move at all, or it moves at the same
5   time as a part of it is at rest. So the rest of one foot is not the
rest of the whole, but of the part. So in walking the whole
moves continuously, and the whole does not come to rest until
both feet come to a halt.

     If walking is continuous and uninterrupted, then, the
walker through void from Athens to Thebes will be in Athens
10   and Thebes at the same time if he is going to get from Athens
to Thebes in no time. But that is impossible, since that way
one could be everywhere at the same time. So either it will be
altogether impossible to walk through void from Athens to
Thebes, or else walking will always be in time. But it does not
make sense that one cannot walk through a void. For what
will there be to prevent one walking, if there is a void? As it is,
15   there is a bodily medium and we part it in walking, but we are
not prevented from walking nevertheless: so why would we
not walk all the more when there is nothing in the way? And
whatever was there to prevent one walking slower and
another faster through void? As it is, when motion takes place
through a body, the one who can move fastest is not
prevented, because the air is easily parted: so if the medium is
20   void, how much less hindrance should there be, and for one
who wants to walk quite slowly? Maybe the bodily medium
would be a hindrance to fast motion, because it has to be
parted, but how could the void be a hindrance to the slower
walk? So if it is possible to walk rather slowly through void,
and slower walking results from happening in a longer time,
25   it is clear that walking through void happened in time. So

what prevents natural motion also from happening in a void?

(c) Again, one might also be convinced of this from motions that are forced and contrary to nature. Suppose two archers shoot in a void, and one is a weak child, the other a very powerful man, and suppose they shoot at a mark the child is able to reach with his arrow. If they release their arrows at 30 the same time, will both arrows touch the mark at the same time and the stronger man's not get there first? Absurd! In that case the stronger power would be contributing nothing to faster shooting, and that is absurd. But if the one shot by the 693,1 stronger power has an advantage, plainly it must be an advantage in time; so the arrow shot by the child will take longer to reach the mark. So if I take a power still stronger than the stronger one, obviously it will have still more 5 advantage – so an advantage in time. So that power, too, took time to move the arrow.

Again, if there were a void, and I threw a stone upwards against nature, would it reach a certain place – say, a stade away – in no time? In that case, if someone stronger threw it it would reach the same place more quickly. But what is quicker than no time? And if it covered this stade in no time, why not 10 two? And so on all the way to the sphere of fixed stars. What is more ridiculous than that? Hence, if these propositions are absurd, it is obvious that even if there were a void, motion contrary to nature would in all cases be in time.

Now, if motions of choice against nature would take time if there is a void, obviously so would natural motions. Let it be assumed that the space between earth and heaven is void: if a stone were released from the sphere of the stars, would it 15 reach earth without lapse of time? What is more ridiculous than this – that the stone should be incommensurably faster than the sphere of stars itself? But if, in no time, either the stone thrown from below reached the uppermost position, or the one from above reached the lowermost (I mean the sphere of stars and the earth respectively), it will follow that the stone is up and down at the same instant, which is impossible. 20 Hence the stone released from above, when the intermediate space is void, must necessarily either not move at all but remain at rest throughout, being raised up in the void into its unnatural place, or, if that again is impossible, it remains that in a certain time it regains its natural place, namely, the earth. So, of three necessary consequences – either the same thing is both up and down at the same time, or the stone remains in its unnatural place raised up in the void, or it moves in time – if the two former have been shown to be impossible, it remains that the third is true.

(d) I believe, then, that it has been shown well enough that, even if there were a void, nothing would prevent the occurrence of motion – motion in time, since there is no timeless motion; but that the occurrence of motion is totally impossible without void can be learnt as follows. Suppose that when motion occurs through a bodily medium such as air the parts of the air must always move aside to yield to the moving thing, and the mass of air displaced must be as great as the moving thing, and that there is no void extension that has received the body displaced by the moving thing – the body that gave room for moving to the moving thing by yielding to it – but the displaced air has vacated no extension: then why was the displacement needed? So that *what* might yield to the moving thing? Not just a surface, of course,[21] since the moving thing is not a surface, so that it could be made room for by a surface by coinciding with it.[22] Body does not coincide with surface. For if the moving thing always exchanges a certain extension equal to itself, and this extension must necessarily either be a body or void, and it is impossible for body to pass through body, it follows that the extensions it occupies successively are void. For if the moving thing is three-dimensional, and it moves wholly, as a whole, obviously it will require a space as great as itself. If that were not so, it would not be the case that a quantity of air as great as itself must be displaced by it. Say it is a cubit, in all three dimensions: then it will need that amount of space. But the void is that space. So it is impossible for motion to occur without void.

Again, if you think of the air displaced by it as shifting from

_____

[21] I do not understand the accusative *epiphaneian*. Perhaps it is a scribe's error for the nominative, as David Sedley suggests (in *Philoponus and the Rejection of Aristotelian Science*, 142).

[22] See the *Corollary on Place* 558,3-10 with note.

its own place without being replaced there by the moving body or by the entrance of the surrounding air, what else would the interval in the surrounding air be except a void extension into 15 which the moving body moves? We have dealt with these subjects more extensively in our discussion of place.[23] It is obvious from this too, then, that the thing moving in place occupies first one void space and then another. I have often indicated that the void is this space, even though – while I assert that it has existence in its own right and definition, and 20 that first one body and then another comes to be in it while it remains immovable – I claim nevertheless that it never remains without body, any more than matter does without form, or body without quality, while yet having their own existence in their proper definition. Just so, then, the void, although having its own existence, is never without body. For air, being fluid and easily moved, never allows a void space to 25 be left, but takes the place of the bodies too quickly before void space is left.

So much, then, for that subject. If someone raises a question about the causes of the different motion of bodies of different shape – what is the ratio in which a ball will fall faster than a 30 flat object when they move in a void? – we shall reply that when the motion takes place in bodily media this is true, and a flat weight with an equal impulse falls more slowly because it is held up by more air, and the same weight parts more air more slowly. But if the motion took place in a void, the 695,1 difference between the faster and the slower will depend entirely on the inequality of their impulses, while the difference in their shapes will make no difference, and the flat thing and the ball, if they have equal impulse, will fall in the same time. For there is nothing to offer more or less 5 hindrance: it is only their natural impulse that activates them to motion. So if their natural impulse is equal and similar, and nothing offers more or less hindrance, their motion must be equal and similar.

[23] *Corollary on Place*. Perhaps 567,8ff., but there are many passages he might have in mind.

English-Greek Glossary

absurd: *atopos*
accept: *paradekhesthai*
accidentally: *kata sumbebêkos*
act, be acted on: *poiein, paskhein*
active: *poiêtikos*
actuality: *energeia*
add: *parathesthai*
affection: *pathos*
agree: *homologein, sunkhôrein*
agreement: *homologêma, homologia*
aim: *skopos*
air: *pneuma*
aloft: *meteôros*
alter: *alloioun*
alteration: *alloiôsis*
apply to: *epharmozein*
approach: *engizein, prosengizein*
argument: *epikheirêma*
argument or definition: *logos*
as expected: *eikotôs*
assumption: *thesis*
axiom: *axiôma*

base: *puthmên*
befall: *hupopiptein*
beginning or principle: *arkhê*
being: *ousia*
bend (v): *epikamptein*
bend (n): *kampsis*
black: *melas*
blacken: *melainein*
boat: *ploion*
bodiliness: *sômatotês*
body: *sôma*
body-extension: *sômatikon diastêma*
bone: *ostoun*

breadth: *platos*
breaking off: *aporrêxis*
bring with: *metagein*
bronze: *khalkos*
burst: *rhêgnunai*

capable of being acted on: *pathêtikos*
category: *katêgoria*
cause: *aition*
centre: *kentron*
change (n): *alloiôsis*
change (v), alter: *metastrephein, alloioun*
change place: *metabainein*
circle: *kuklos*
circular motion: *periphora*
claim (v): *axioun, prospoieisthai*
clear: *saphês*
clepsydra: *klepsudra*
collapse: *sumpiptein*
come to be in: *engignesthai*
common: *koinos*
common opinion: *koinê ennoia*
concave: *kurtos*
conceal: *perikaluptein*
confuse: *kukoun*
confusion: *sunkhusis*
conjoin: *sunaptein*
contain, surround: *periekhein, emperiekhein*
continuity: *sunekheia*
continuous: *sunekhês*
contradict: *antilegein*
contrary to nature: *para phusin*
contribute: *suntelein*
cosmic: *kosmikos*
cosmos: *kosmos*
create: *dêmiourgein*
creator: *dêmiourgos*
crookedness: *skoliotês*
cube: *kubos*
cubit: *pêkhus*; one cubit long: *pêkhuaios*
cut through: *diakoptein, temnein*
cut, divide: *temnein*

danger: *kindunos*
defeat (v): *nikan*
defence: *apologia*
defend: *apologeisthai*

deficient: *katadeês*
define, limit: *horizein*
defining: *horistikos*
definition: *horismos, horos, logos*
demonstrate: *apodeiknunai*
demonstration: *apodeixis*
denial: *anairesis*
dense: *puknos*
density: *puknotês*
deny: *arneisthai*
deny, do away with: *anairein*
depth: *bathos*
destroy along with: *sumphtheirein*
destructible: *phthartos*
detach: *apospazein*
determine: *aphorizein*
dice: *kuboi*
difference: *diaphora*
different: *diaphoros*
difficulty: *aporia*
dimension: *diastasis*
diminution: *meiôsis*
displaced, be: *antimethistanai*
dispose, set in order: *dioikein*
distinguish: *diorizein*
distribute: *epinemein*
divide: *diairein, temnein*
division: *diairesis, tomê*
doubt or difficulty: *aporia*
down: *katô*
downward moving: *katôpheres*
drain off: *exantlein*
draw: *anazôigraphein*
draw out with: *sunelkuein*

earth: *gê*
easy: *eukolos*
eject: *ekballein*
entrance: *eisodos, pareisdusis*
equal: *isos*
examination: *episkepsis*
examine: *episkeptesthai*
excess: *huperbolê*
exchange (v): *ameibein*
exchange (n): *ameipsis, antimetastasis*
exist in: *enuparkhein*
exit: *diexodos*

expend: *dapanan*
extended in two dimensions: *dikhêi diastaton*
extension: *diastêma*

fallacy: *paralogismos*
falsity: *pseudos*
famous: *poluthrulêtos*
father: *patêr*
female: *thêlus*
fictitious: *plasmatôdês*
fill: *plêroun*
filling: *plêrôsis*
fine: *leptos*
fine-grained: *leptomerês*
fire: *pur*
fixed: *aplanês* (of the sphere of fixed stars)
flesh: *sarx*
float, be supported on: *epokheisthai, epipolazein*
follow: *akolouthein*
food: *trophê*
foolish: *euêthês*
force (v): *biazein*
force, rush (n): *rhumê*
force of the void: *bia tou kenou*
form: *eidos*
forwards: *prosô*
full: *nastos*

get out from under: *hupexistasthai*
go well: *euodein*
god: *theos*
gold: *khrusos*
grape-juice: *gleukos*

hardness: *sklêrotês*
harm: *blaptein*
harmonious: *sumphônos*
heat: *thermotês*
heaven: *ouranos*
heaviness: *barutês*
heavy: *barus*
high: *hupsêlos*
hinder, prevent: *kôluein*
hollow: *koilos*
honey: *meli*
house-building: *oikodomia*
hypothesis: *hupothesis*

hypothesise: *hupotithenai*

implication: *sumplokê*
impulse: *hormê, rhopê*
in itself: *kath' hauto*
inch: *daktulos*
increase: *auxêsis*
inert: *apathês*
inflate: *phusan*
inflow: *eisrhoê*
inquire, examine: *episkeptesthai*
inquiry, examination: *episkepsis*
interior: *entos*
interpreter: *exêgêtês*
invent: *plattein*
irrational: *alogos*

jar: *amphoreus, pithos*

keep: *phulattein*

last: *eskhatos*
lead (n): *molibdos*
least: *elakhistos*
leave behind: *katalimpanein*
length: *mêkos*
light: *kouphos*
like: *homoios*
limit (v): *horizein, perainein*
limit (n): *peras*
limited, be: *peratousthai, sumperatousthai*
line: *grammê*
living: *zôos*
living creature: *zôon*
long: *makros*
lottery: *apoklêrôsis*
lunar sphere: *selêniakê sphaira*

magnitude: *megethos*
make finer: *leptunein*
make up, invent: *plattein*
male: *arrên*
measure (n): *metron*
measure (v): *metrein*
meltable: *têktos*
moist: *hugros*
motion: *phora*

mountain: *oros*
mouth: *opê, stoma, stomion*
move: *kinein*
move along with: *summetapherein*
move aside to yield: *antiparakhôrein*
move forwards: *proienai*
move, pass: *khôrein*

naked: *gumnos*
natural, physical: *phusikos*
natural philosopher: *phusiologos*
necessary: *anankaios*
necessitate: *anankazein*
necessity: *anankê*
next in order: *ephexês*
northern: *arktôios*

object (v): *hupantan, enistasthai, enkalein*
obstinate, be: *prosphiloneikein*
occupy: *katekhein*
occur: *sumbainein*
opinion: *dogma*
opposite: *enantios*
opposite to, be: *antikeisthai*
order: *taxis*
originable: *genêtos*
outermost: *exôtatô*
outline: *perigraphein*
own definition: *idios logos*
own nature: *idia phusis*

part: *morion*
pass: *khôrein*
pass through a body: *khôrein (kineisthai) dia sômatos*
passing: *khôrêsis*
perfection: *teleiotês*
perforation: *trêma*
perimeter: *perimetros*
periphery: *periphereia*
persuade: *peithein*
physical: *phusikos*
pipe: *aulos*
place: *topos*
place-extension: *topikon diastêma*
plausible: *pithanos*
play dice: *petteuein*
pole: *polos*

pore: *poros*
postulate (n): *aitêma*
pot: *keramos, ostrakon*
power: *dunamis*
preserve, keep: *sôizein, phulattein*
prevent: *kôluein*
principle: *arkhê*
proper place: *oikeios topos*
push back: *antôthein*
put on top of: *epitithenai*

quality: *poiotês*
quality (category): *poion*
quality-less: *apoios*
quantity (category): *poson*
quotation: *lexis*

raise another objection: *epaporein*
random: *apoklêrôtikos, tukhôn*
rational: *logikos*
reasonable: *eulogos*
reasonable, be: *noun exein*
reasoning: *epikheirêsis*
receptive: *dektikos*
refutation: *elenkhos*
refute: *elenkhein*
reject: *apodokimazein*
relation: *skhesis*
relax: *khalazein*
remember, recall: *anamnêsthenai*
remove: *aphistan, exairein*
resemble: *exomoioun*
resistance: *antitupia*
response: *apantêsis*
rest: *êremia, stasis*
ridiculous: *geloion*
risk: *kinduneuein*
river: *potamos*
rotation: *dinêsis*
rush: *rhumê*
rush in instead: *antempiptein*

sea: *thalassa*
seduce: *sunarpazein*
self-subsistent: *authupostatos*
separable: *khôristos*
set in order: *dioikein, kosmein*

shape: *skhêma*
size, magnitude: *megethos*
smallness: *smikrotês*
softness: *malakotês*
solid: *stereos*
somewhat empty: *hupokenos*
son: *huios*
soul: *psukhê*
south: *notios*
space: *khôra*
sphere: *sphaira*
(one) stade long: *stadiaion*
stand out: *existasthai*
stay in place: *menein*
steal: *kleptein*
sticky: *gliskhros*
stone: *lithos*
stop up: *apophrassein, ekphrassein*
straight line, in a: *kat' eutheian*
stretch out: *ekteinein*
stronger: *kreittôn*
subsist: *huphistanai*
suck out: *ekmuzan*
suck up: *anarrophein*
sufficient: *hikanos*
summit: *koruphê*
surface: *embadon, epiphaneia*
surround, contain: *periekhein, emperiekhein*
sweet: *glukus*

take away: *huphairein*
take out, remove: *exairein*
ten thousand: *murioi*
tending to move upwards: *anôphoros*
theorem: *theôrêma*
think of: *ennoein, theôrein*
third: *tritos*
thought, in: *kat' epinoian*
three-dimensional: *trikhêi diastaton*
through the whole: *di' holou*
time: *khronos*
touch: *haptesthai*
treatise: *pragmateia*
true: *alêthês*
truth: *alêtheia*

unchangeable: *ametablêtos*

Greek-English Index

References are to the page and line numbers in the margins of the translation.

Subject Index

SIMPLICIUS

Against Philoponus
On the Eternity of the World

translated by
Christian Wildberg

Introduction

Part I
Richard Sorabji

The content and reliability of Simplicius' report

In the sixth century AD Philoponus wrote a series of treatises supporting the Christian rejection of the eternity of the world. Details are given below. One treatise, or a part of it, is summarised and attacked by the pagan Neoplatonist Simplicius in the passage translated here by Christian Wildberg. The text casts a light, to my mind unfavourable, on Simplicius as a reporter of his enemy Philoponus.

Simplicius records five groups of arguments. They are concerned more obviously with the world's ending rather than with its beginning. The first exploits Aristotle's concession of the world's finite capacity. The others provide Philoponus' own arguments.

(i) 1327,11. *Aristotle's denial to finite bodies of infinite capacity proves the world perishable.* Aristotle had argued that all body, being finite in size, has only finite capacity. Hence the infinite cause needed for the eternal motion of the heavens is neither a body, nor housed in a body. It is rather God.

Philoponus uses the world's finite capacity to infer instead its perishability. But he is perfectly well aware, as his subsequent arguments (and his other treatises)[1] show, that this can only be an opening move, because others will reply that the infinite capacity needed to stop the world perishing is housed in God.

---

[1] For the relevance of these, see Richard Sorabji, *Matter, Space and Motion*, London and Ithaca NY 1988, ch. 15.

Simplicius assumes this as part of his own answer without acknowledging that Philoponus goes on to recognise it. But he makes a further point of some value. Someone, whether Philoponus or Simplicius, had raised the question whether the world does not need an infinite capacity correlative to God's capacity to move it and keep it in being. Simplicius replies that it does not, in any unacceptable sense. For God's infinite capacity exists in him all at once. But all the world needs at any time is a *finite* capacity to be moved and kept in being for that time. If this is also an infinite capacity, it is so only in the weak sense of being renewable without limit.

We are next given arguments by Philoponus that do not rest on Aristotle's concessions. Simplicius represents these too as arguing from finite capacity to perishability, although their structure, as he reports it, seems more varied than this.

(ii) 1329, 19. *Its dependence on matter proves the world of finite capacity and hence perishable so far as its own nature is concerned.* Philoponus treats finite capacity as necessary and sufficient for perishability (Simplicius later says 'identical with' it: 1333,34). But what Simplicius does not acknowledge, or treats when he mentions it as merely a case of forgetting (1331,27), is that Philoponus deliberately shifts his ground. If somebody says that God can override the world's finite capacity and tendency to perish, at least it should be conceded that it is of finite capacity and perishable 'so far as its own nature is concerned' (1329,33). The point is not explicitly made until 1331,7 (see iv.a below) but the terminology already crops up here.

(iii) 1329,33: *The world is perishable because matter requires changes of form.* In his reply to this next argument, Simplicius is unaware that what Philoponus views as the prime matter common to the heavens and our part of the universe is three-dimensional extension.[2] The prime matter of the heavens is not, for Philoponus, Aristotle's fifth element.

---

[2] Sorabji, *Matter, Space and Motion*, ch. 2, and (ed) *Philoponus and the Rejection of Aristotelian Science*, ch. 1; Christian Wildberg, *John Philoponus' Criticism of Aristotle's Theory of Aether*, Berlin and New York 1988, ch. 7.2.

(iv.a) 1331,7: *Even if God can override the world's natural tendency to perish, it is still perishable so far as its own nature is concerned.* This is the deliberate shift of ground which Simplicius dismisses as mere forgetting. Simplicius' treatment will be all the less justified if it is the *same* text of Philoponus which he and Pines' Arabic summary are reporting. For we know from the Arabic that Philoponus went on to argue further that God could not override the world's natural tendency to begin and make it beginningless, even if he could override its natural tendency to perish. None of this is reported by Simplicius.

(iv.b) 1332,3: *That bodies are perishable and have a finite capacity so far as their own nature is concerned can be shown by their divisibility into parts which are perishable and of finite capacity.* This is treated as a continuation of the same argument. Simplicius admits he is paraphrasing (*skhedon,* 1332,27). So we must be careful about what the editor, Diels, has chosen to present as if it were direct quotation from Philoponus.[3] Certainly, some of the argument depends on the idea of perishability with no obvious reference to finite capacity.

Simplicius does, however, have an important reply to Philoponus: the world's nature is not simply overriden if it is preserved forever by God, because it must be part of its nature to be able to receive this gift.

Simplicius also probes the relationship between our being able to *imagine* perishing, and perishing being possible, and between its possibility and its actually happening in the course of infinite time. But to make his first point, Simplicius has to alter what Philoponus actually says (1334,29). And as regards the second point, Philoponus surely intends an answer to his question, 'from what source is it that this being of a nature to be destroyed will never come to be actualised?' (1334,37-9). The answer acknowledged throughout argument (iv) is: God.

(v) 1335,17: *The whole has finite capacity because the parts have, as is shown (a) by their own dependence on the whole, (b) by the fact that they must be smaller than the whole.* Simplicius

---

[3] Christian Wildberg tells me that MS A has no quotation marks at this point.

finishes with a criticism of this argument. Altogether he reports considerably fewer arguments than the Arabic summary, but he gives them a detailed discussion.

Part II
Christian Wildberg

Philoponus' treatises on the world's perishability

In the middle period of his life, Philoponus devoted himself to the project of lending philosophical respectability to the Christian doctrine that the universe, being the creation of God, is perishable and not, as Aristotle so influentially argued, indestructible and eternal. At least three major treatises date from this time: the *de Aeternitate Mundi contra Proclum,* completed in 529;[4] the *de Aeternitate Mundi contra Aristotelem,* written between 530 and 534 and extant only in fragments;[5] and finally a work apparently entitled *de Contingentia Mundi* which was not directed against any particular philosopher.[6] It is not possible to say with certainty whether Simplicius, in the pages of his *Physics* commentary translated here, is in fact discussing the first part of that treatise. Independent evidence suggests that Simplicius had before him yet another work, a smaller and more specific pamphlet on the subject *That each body is finite and possesses finite capacity.*[7] Whichever work it was that Simplicius had a copy of, it is clear that it was composed after the *contra Aristotelem* had been published because Philoponus explicitly refers to that treatise. A precise absolute date is indeterminable.

---

[4] Edited by H. Rabe, Leipzig 1899.

[5] Translation in this series of the surviving fragments by C. Wildberg, *Philoponus: Against Aristotle on the Eternity of the World,* London and Ithaca N.Y. 1987.

[6] There exist Arabic abstracts of this work, see S. Pines, 'An Arabic summary of a lost work of John Philoponus', in *Israel Oriental Studies* 2 (1972), 320-52; G. Troupeau, 'Un épitomé arabe du *de Contingentia Mundi* de Jean Philopon', in Memorial A.J. Festugière, *Cahiers d'orientalisme* 10 (1984), 77-88.

[7] A treatise like that consisting of just one book appears in the Arabic bibliographies of Ibn al-Nadîm, Ibn al-Qiftî and Ibn Abî Uṣaybiʻa; cf. e.g. M. Steinschneider, 'Johannes Philoponus bei den Arabern', in *Al-Farabi – Alpharabius – des arabischen Philosophen Leben und Schriften, Mémoires de l'academie impériale des sciences de St. Pétersbourg,* série 7, XIII 4 (1869), 162; F. Sezgin, *Geschichte des Arabischen Schrifttums,* Leiden 1970, vol. 3, 157-60.

The character of Philoponus' argument

In the first two polemical treatises just mentioned the strategy most widely used by Philoponus is to turn the opponent's arguments against him. This is very similar to what he is in fact doing in the treatise discussed by Simplicius here. Philoponus draws on a passage of Aristotle which is included in the latter's proof that the ultimate cause of motion has no bodily magnitude (*Phys.* 8.10). Aristotle here argues here that no finite magnitude can possess an infinite *dunamis* (266a23-b6). This argument, which John Philoponus exploited for quite different purposes some 880 years later, may be paraphrased like this:

> Grant that a greater *dunamis* always produces the same change in a less time. A finite magnitude with an infinite *dunamis* would necessarily produce a very great change, but this change could not possibly take any time. For if it took a certain time, one could conceive of a finite *dunamis* which, sufficiently incremented, could produce the same change in precisely the same time as it took the infinite *dunamis*; but this is impossible. Hence, no finite magnitude possesses an infinite *dunamis*.

An important feature of this argument is the meaning of the word *dunamis*. The topic of Aristotle's chapter is motion and its first cause, and one can safely assume that *dunamis* has the sense of 'principle of motion and change' (according to the first definition of the term in *Metaph.* 5.12) or even 'kinetic force'.[8] In Philoponus, as will be seen, the term is given a much wider meaning, and the argument is taken to establish a quite different conclusion.

Simplicius represents Philoponus as having made two points and (1327,14-16; 1328,33-5; 1329,17-19 and 22-4; 1333,34f) as having inferred one from the other. If this is right, he will first have corroborated Aristotle's tenet of the impossibility of an infinite capacity in a finite magnitude by a

---

[8] Cf. the term *dunamis tou kinein* in the discussion of projectile motion, *Phys.* 8.10, 267a8f. *dunamis* is used in this sense too in the notorious chapter 7.5, where it is a synonym of *iskhus*.

number of independent arguments. On the strength of this he will then have inferred that the world must be perishable, a conclusion which of course runs counter to Aristotelian doctrine. It is not entirely clear how much Philoponus felt entitled to claim, whether it was that 'the world *can* cease to exist' or that 'the world *will* cease to exist'. Undoubtedly he holds that the world, being a finite body, has only finite capacity by nature and that this is a necessary and sufficient condition for it being perishable as far as depends on it. Thus he appears to concede that the will of God may very well prevent it from actual decay.[9] But other passages in Simplicius' report suggest that he went a step further and claimed that finite capacity is also a necessary and sufficient condition for the world's *actual* destruction in the future, regardless of the will of God.[10] If we can believe Simplicius on this, then Philoponus could have found strong support in Alexander of Aphrodisias,[11] although one finds no indication in Simplicius' polemic that he did refer to him.

But why should Aristotle's argument in *Phys.* 8.10 render such sweeping metaphysical conclusions? The main reason, I take it, is that Philoponus understands and uses the term *dunamis* in a different sense. Aristotle was concerned with *motion*, and in his argument *dunamis* had the sense of 'kinetic force'; Philoponus is concerned with *being* and holds that the mere existence of a thing requires of it the possession of a *dunamis* which saves it from disintegration and decay. This becomes clear at 1335,38f. where Philoponus is reported to speak of a *dunamis* that is *sunektikê tou einai dunamis*, a term which betrays Stoic influence.[12] Like any force or capacity, this *dunamis* is necessarily exhausted in the course of time, so that

---

[9] This would agree with remarks in the Arabic abstracts, see Pines, 324 and Troupeau, 84.

[10] 1333,27-30; 1334,34-1335,16; indirectly 1336,3-5.

[11] Who argued in *Quaestiones* 1.18 that the world cannot be imperishable because of the will of God if it is perishable by its own nature; see I. Bruns (ed.), *Alexandri Aphrodisiensis praeter commentaria scripta minora*, Supplementum Aristotelicum II(2), Berlin 1892, 30-2.

[12] cf. below note 58 ad loc. I am grateful to Richard Sorabji for the point. Cf. also J.E. McGuire, 'Philoponus on *Physics* II 1: *physis, hormê emphutos* and the motion of simple bodies', *Ancient Philosophy* (1985), 241- 67.

every finite body, including the celestial, must be regarded as perishable by nature.[13]

The manuscripts

Only a few of the extant manuscripts of Simplicius' *Physics* commentary have the complete text of his comments on book 8; most of them break off well before they get to the section translated here.[14] I was able to compare the *CAG* text with two important manuscripts, the oldest witness Marcianus gr. 226 of the ninth century (MS A) and the much younger Marcianus gr. 219 of the fifteenth century (MS G).[15] Variant readings adopted in the translation are both listed on p. 104 and recorded at the place of their occurrence in the text. In the translation, angle brackets include words that do not occur in the original Greek; round brackets enclose parentheses. Inverted commas are used to indicate passages in which Simplicius reports Philoponus' views; they are not meant to suggest that the lines are verbatim quotations from Philoponus' treatise.

Finally, I would like to thank Richard Sorabji and John Ellis for their constructive criticism and advice.

---

[13] On Philoponus' influence on mediaeval proofs of creation see H.A. Davidson, 'John Philoponus as a source of medieval Islamic and Jewish proofs of creation', in *Journal of the American Oriental Society* 89 (1969), 357-91, esp. 362ff.

[14] On the textual transmission of Simplicius' *Physics* commentary see D. Harlfinger, 'Einige Aspekte der handschriftlichen Überlieferung des Physikkommentars des Simplikios', in I. Hadot (ed.), *Simplicius: sa vie, son oeuvre, sa survie*, Berlin and New York 1987, 267-86.

[15] The fact that at 1330,30 MS G reads correctly *ta ourania* where MS A has the obviously false *ta hoti* suggests that G is an independent witness.

Textual emendations

The following departures from Diels' text on pages 1326-36 of Simplicius' *Physics* commentary have been adopted in this translation.

1327,5   Punctuating with full stop after *tote* with MS A.
1327,26-29 *ex hôn ... ekhousan dunamin* in quotation marks with MS A.
1331,10   Reading *heautôn* for *heautou* with MS A and G.
1332,9   Ending parenthesis after *genoito an*.
1333,28/30 Placing the interrogation mark after *energeian* rather than after *gar*.
1334,26   Reading *houtos* for *houtôs* with the Aldine edition.
1336,16   Rejecting the proposed emendation <*osta*>.

SIMPLICIUS

Against Philoponus
On the Eternity of the World

Translation

Simplicius against Philoponus on Aristotle's argument that no infinite capacity can reside in a finite body

(Simplicius *in Phys.* 1326,38-1336,34)

But this Grammarian[1] whom I <sc. Simplicius> mentioned at the beginning of the lectures on this book[2] regarded it as a matter of great importance if he could entice large numbers of laymen to disparage the heavens and the whole world as 1327,1 things that are just as perishable as themselves, and evidently to <disparage> the world's divine craftsman (*dêmiourgos*) as well if he were demonstrably a maker of a generated and perishable world who in all of time before he created was no creator nor God, father, and supporter (*hupostatês*) of everything that exists. For nothing that is 5 <now> had even come to be then.[3] Starting from such gigantic conceptions this gentleman not only dared to write against Aristotle's arguments in the first <book> of *On the Heavens* concerning the eternity of the heavens and the world – without understanding what the text says, as I have attempted to demonstrate in the respective <lectures>.[4] He

---

[1] Simplicius refers to his Alexandrian colleague in two ways: most frequently he simply uses *houtos*, 'this man', but occasionally, as in the present passage, he uses *ho Grammatikos*, 'the grammarian or philologist'. The former way is evidently meant to be rude, whereas the second is an epithet Simplicius has apparently taken over from Philoponus himself (cf. *in Cael.* 119,7); nevertheless, the intended connotation may very well be that Philoponus is not a proper philosopher like, e.g., Porphyry, Proclus or Damascius (cf. *CAG*, Index of Names s.v. *Grammatikos*).

[2] i.e. Aristotle's *Physics*, book 8 and Simplicius *in Phys.* 1117,15-1118,11. In that commentary (pp. 1129-82) Simplicius discusses Philoponus' criticism of Aristotle's arguments for the eternity of motion and time in *Physics* 8.1. I have offered a translation of Philoponus' arguments in *Philoponus: Against Aristotle on the Eternity of the World*, London and Ithaca N.Y. 1987, 122-46.

[3] Full stop after *tote* with MS A.

[4] See Simplicius *in Cael.* 26-199 passim.

also opposed the <arguments> at the beginning of this book
10   <i.e. *Physics* 8> which show that motion and time are eternal
(*aïdia*); his objections are beside the point, as one can clearly
grasp from my replies to him.[5]

<In Simplicius' view, Aristotle's denial to finite bodies of
infinite capacity[6] is misused by Philoponus to prove the
world perishable.>

Now he thought that he was also helped towards this same
purpose (*skopos*) by the Aristotelian proof by which
<Aristotle> shows that no finite body possesses an infinite
capacity[7] (*ouden sôma peperasmenon apeiron ekhei dunamin*).
For if both the body that makes up the celestial region and the
15   body of the whole universe are finite, they possess a finite
capacity; but that which possesses a finite capacity is, as this
<Grammarian> thinks, immediately shown to be perishable.
And indeed, at the end of the argument he states: 'It remains
<to conclude> that heaven as a whole as well as each of its
parts possesses a finite capacity; but the same is true of all the
things below the moon too.' Remarkable that he did not add
20   that this is also true of himself; for the whole intention of
these people's[8] (*autôn*) piety is to show that both the heavens
and the heavens' creator do not differ from them in any
respect.
   To my mind it is important that those who encounter the
<Grammarian's> arguments understand that in the present

---

[5] Simplicius is referring to his earlier discussion of Philoponus' arguments, cf. *in Phys.* 1117ff.

[6] Aristotle argues at *Phys.* 8.9, 266a23-b6 that it is impossible for an infinite capacity to reside in a finite magnitude; he then uses the finite capacity of all body to show that the cause of the eternal motion of the heavens is neither a body nor housed in a body. Philoponus appropriates this argument to show that the world, being a finite body, must be perishable. There is evidence that this was only his opening move and that he knew he had to meet counterarguments. Simplicius does not acknowledge this. See R. Sorabji, *Matter, Space and Motion,* London and Ithaca N.Y. 1988, ch. 15 and p. 112 below. Simplicius here argues that Philoponus cannot infer the world's perishability from its finite capacity. For all the world needs at any time is a *finite* capacity (renewable ad infinitum) to be moved for that length of time. There is indeed an infinite capacity which exists all at once, but this is the capacity for *causing* motion, and it exists in the divine mover, who, being incorporeal, can accommodate it.

[7] The Greek word *dunamis* is consistently translated 'capacity' in order not to commit the translation to either 'force' or 'potentiality'.

[8] i.e. the Christians.

context too he is clearly not following Aristotle's text and is ignorant of their overall purpose. For he thinks that Aristotle held that the possession of an infinite capacity to cause motion 25 (*dunamin apeiron kinêtikên*) is identical with the capacity to remain in a state of being moved for an infinite time. And indeed, <the Grammarian> writes this:[9] '<...> from which it has been made clear to us that Aristotle regarded it as true that no finite body possesses a capacity which lasts for an infinite time. Whence <the Grammarian> states that a capacity which has its being in a body can cause the eternal motion.'[10] And he did not understand that having an infinite 30 capacity all at once which is capable of causing eternal motion is different from being able to remain eternally in a state of being moved; and that in the first instance an actual infinite capacity belongs to the eternal mover all at once, whereas in the second instance the infinite – in the sense of being capable of being moved for ever (*ep' apeiron*), not in virtue of the active capacity to cause motion, which exists all at once, but in virtue of the passive <capacity> and potential (*to dunamei*) – 35 belongs to that which is being moved eternally. Alexander, too, whom this man cites, says at the end of his comments on this book (i.e. *Physics* 8) that in the case of something being moved for ever one cannot speak of a capacity in virtue of which it is being moved, except homonymously.[11] Hence, an infinite capacity existing all at once to cause motion cannot possibly belong to a finite body, but nothing prevents motion 40

[9] In the margin of both manuscripts Marcianus 226 (A) and Marcianus 219 (G) the two following sentences are clearly marked as a quotation (fol. 349ᵛ and 332ᵛ resp.). The 'us' in the first sentence must then be referring to Philoponus.

[10] As it stands, the second sentence seems to suggest that Philoponus' statement presupposed the fundamental assumption of impetus theory that capacities or motive forces always reside *in* the body which undergoes motion, and are not external to it. Thus, all that Philoponus is trying to get out of the Aristotelian passage at this point is the concession that if there is such a thing that moves eternally it must itself be in the possession of a infinite *dunamis* which facilitates this. He ignores the distinction between active and passive capacities (which infuriates Simplicius) and simply proceeds to draw the conclusion reported at 1328,7-9 below.

Alternatively, Philoponus, still being quoted by Simplicius, could just be referring to two sentences in Aristotle (the implied subject of *phêsin*), viz. *Phys.* 8.10, 266a23-26. But in that case one must suppose that a 'not' has been dropped out (perhaps one should read *oude* for *hothen*?): 'And <Aristotle> states that a capacity which has its being in a body cannot cause the eternal motion.' (I am grateful to Eric Lewis for this suggestion).

[11] Simplicius reports Alexander's position again later on in his commentary at 1358,18ff.

ad infinitum from belonging to a finite <body> because taken
at any moment the capacity used in what undergoes infinite
motion is finite.[12] Clearly, it is not necessary that there be a
pause while one <capacity> succeeds the other, both because
of the eternal mover and because of the inherence
(*hupoikouria*) of the potential (*to dunamei*) which resides at
any moment in that which is being moved. So in this context
<the Grammarian> is ignorant, just as he was before, of the
difference between what is infinite all at once (*to hama holon
on apeiron*) and ad infinitum infinity (*to ep' apeiron*), which is
also infinite and lasts eternally; <he ignores> that the one
properly belongs to the eternal mover, the other to that which
is being eternally moved.

Because of this ignorance he thought that one who shows
that in a finite body there is no infinite capacity all at once to
cause motion has shown by this that a finite body cannot be
moved for ever; for he is unaware of what Aristotle said in the
third <book> of this treatise <i.e. *Physics* 3> about ad
infinitum infinity, some of which I <sc. Simplicius> have
cited at the beginning of my lectures on this book, some I shall
cite now: '*For in general, the infinite is like this because one
thing is always being taken after another, and whatever is
taken is always finite, but it is always something else.*'[13]
<Infinity> of this sort belongs to things that possess being in
<a chain of> generation. For motion and time and the
generation of mankind are of this sort (as Aristotle states as
well) and the division of magnitudes. For because motion
takes place in the moved object and not in the mover, as has
been shown in the arguments on motion,[14] it is necessary that
the prime mover, which is always unmoved, possess an
infinite capacity because it <is a mover> always, and <the
capacity> is indeed infinite in the sense of being all at once.
For if it were something which was moved on account of a
growing infinity (*hê ginomenê apeiria*) and were not a mover

1328,1

5

10

15

20

---

[12] Over any period of time, the capacity for being moved throughout that period is
finite. It is infinite ad infinitum, i.e. merely in the sense that it can be forever
renewed.

[13] See *Phys.* 3.6, 206a27-9. The idea is that one can always take one more number,
or division, or day, or generation, or celestial revolution, in an infinite series, but
what one takes is always finite.

[14] cf. Aristotle *Physics* 3.3.

nor something unmoved, it too would be in need of another mover. But a finite body which is always being moved continues to move ad infinitum not because it possesses an infinite capacity all at once like the mover. For that which always causes motion in the first place is incorporeal (*asômaton*) and self-substantial (*authupostaton*) and the supplier of an infinite capacity to itself; but that which is 25 always being moved is a finite body and obtains for ever being and motion from the prime mover; hence it cannot accept the motion all at once; otherwise it would no longer have to be moved by something else nor would it move at all. For motion is not something that takes place all at once but possesses its being in <a chain of> generation. For if the moved object accepted <the motion> all at once it would stand still and not move.

This, I think, may suffice both on the mover's infinity being 30 all at once, on account of which it cannot be a finite body, and on the change of that which is immediately moved by it ad infinitum. Because the <Grammarian> does not know the difference between these things he thought that what has been shown by Aristotle now – that no finite body possesses an infinite capacity to cause motion – helped him in demonstrating heaven to be perishable. Yet even though he did not 35 understand the difference between causing motion and being moved,[15] and between actual infinity (*to kat' energeian apeiron*) and ad infinitum infinity (*to ep' apeiron*), he should have realised this at any rate, that Aristotle would not have contradicted himself right away in this one book, showing in the beginning that motion necessarily exists always and that what is moved is eternal, showing next that the body which 40 moves with circular motion[16] is capable of being moved with a single, continuous, and eternal motion, but claiming now that 1329,1 heaven is perishable because it has a finite body – assuming that he understood 'not having an infinite capacity' in this way; and again, in the first <book> of *On the Heavens*, which continues the argument of the present book <i.e. *Physics 8*>,

---

[15] Simplicius accuses Philoponus of being confused whereas in fact it is Simplicius who fails to understand that Philoponus views motion as a process which requires the imparting of forces.

[16] i.e. the heavens.

<Aristotle> demonstrates that the heavens and the whole world are manifestly eternal, demonstrations against which
5   this man too thinks he has brought good arguments. Now what kind of chameleon would undergo such changes as this man thought that Aristotle underwent? Moreover, he did not understand that none of Aristotle's commentators thought that the arguments on the eternity of the heavens and what is
10 being shown now needed arbitration. For in these <arguments Aristotle> evidently denied the infinite capacity which exists all at once to cause motion <only> to a body that causes motion and is finite.[17]

The <Grammarian> is ignorant of the whole purpose of the Aristotelian demonstration and thinks that someone who shows that a finite body does not possess an infinite capacity
15 to cause motion would have shown directly that heaven, since it is finite, is perishable; he attempts to show both through this and through his own arguments[18] that a finite body possesses a finite capacity, and he concludes, as if it followed from this with necessity, that heaven is perishable. Now, let us tackle these misconceptions of his.

<The first of Philoponus's own arguments: dependence on matter shows the world of finite capacity and perishable so far as its own nature is concerned.>

20 The first argument he puts forward consists of the following inference: 'The things in heaven consist of matter and form; things that consist of matter need matter for their being; things that are in need of something are not self-sufficient (*autarkê*); things that are not self-sufficient do not possess an infinite capacity.' And he infers from this that the things in heaven do not have an infinite capacity *in virtue of their own nature*[19] and are perishable because of this. But it is evident
25 that the heavens would no doubt be perishable if they needed

---

[17] But not to the incorporeal first mover: God.

[18] These are the four arguments that follow.

[19] Simplicius betrays in this expression that Philoponus was actually aware that there might be an infinite capacity in another nature (God's), and that further argument was therefore needed to prove that the world will actually perish in the future. We know from Philoponus' other treatises that he offered such argument. See Sorabji, *Matter, Space and Motion*, ch. 15.

perishable matter for their being. But if someone claims without being refuted that the matter or the substrate which at any time belongs to them is imperishable, why should that which is in need of an imperishable substrate be regarded as perishable? For it is not the case that just because <heaven> is in need of something and is in this respect not self-sufficient, it is therefore necessarily perishable as well. For that which is not self-substantial (*to mê authupostaton*)   30 would probably not have an infinite capacity but would have its being <dependent> on something else (*en allôi to einai ekhon*). However, it is not at all necessary that it be perishable too in the sense of <actually> perishing at some time <in the future>. For as has been said, the actual infinity which is all at once is different from ad infinitum infinity.

<The second of Philoponus' arguments for perishability: matter requires changes of form.>

'Second, he says: If the essence of matter (*to einai tês hulês*) consists precisely in being suitably apt to receive all forms, and if <matter> does not possess this capacity to no purpose, and if the same <portion of> matter is incapable of accepting   35 several forms at once, then, on account of its own definition, matter cannot sustain (*stegein*) any of the forms for ever (*aei*). But if that is the case, none of the things that consist of matter and form will be imperishable because of matter.'

<First supporting argument:>

He says that in the fourth <book> of the <treatise> *Against Aristotle*[20] he has shown that one and the same prime matter underlies both the heavens and the things below the moon.[21]

---

[20] See fragments 69-72 in Wildberg, *Philoponus: Against Aristotle on the Eternity of the World*, 77-91. Philoponus' argument consisted of several steps. First, he argued that the heavens may be regarded as a compound of celestial form and matter (fr. 69); next, he attacked the Neoplatonic notion of prime matter as incorporeal (fr. 70) and argued finally that the ultimate substratum of both the celestial and the sublunary regions must be three-dimensional extension, *to trikhêi diastaton* (fr. 71-2), which is corporeal.

[21] The alleged common matter was three-dimensional corporeal extension, cf. below n. 29. The relevance is that the matter of the things below the moon indisputably requires change of form; on the assumption of one common matter the

1330,1 But what he uttered there I have met with the examination it deserves when I attempted to interpret the first <book> of *On the Heavens*. In the present context the proper reply is no more than this: that f matter were the same and related to all forms in the same way, then the things in heaven and the

5 things below the moon would necessarily *change into one another;* but what w uld be more impossible than this? It is no good dwelling on th is. For indeed this man entertains the <following> incongi uity:

<Second supporting argument:>

'Even if one conceded, he says, that it is not the same matter which underlies both the things in heaven and the things below the moon, nevertheless, since the matter of all celestial <bodies> which they[22] regard as first substrate, is one single

10 so-called fifth body, and since the forms of this matter are indeed different (take for example the <form> of the sun, of the moon, of each of the other stars and moreover each <form> of the spheres), then it is clear that the matter of the celestial bodies is suitably apt to receive each of the celestial forms, even if, in virtue of some stronger and transcendent cause (*dia tina kreittona kai exêirêmenên aitian*),[23] it did not receive them. So if the matter of the celestial bodies too, in

15 virtue of being capable of accepting all forms, will accept different forms of them at different times, none of the things in heaven will therefore be imperishable in virtue of the capacity of their own matter.'

<Simplicius replies:>

(1) Now with regard to these <arguments> it is first worth bearing in mind that he[24] regarded the fifth body as the prime matter of the heavens; if however, as he stated earlier, there

---

celestial region would necessarily be subject to changes of form as well.

[22] Those who follow Aristotle in positing two ontologically different cosmic regions (celestial and sublunary) and postulate a fifth element other than earth, air, fire, and water as the most fundamental material subject of the heavens.

[23] i.e. God.

[24] Although the statement is true of Aristotle, Simplicius seems to be referring to Philoponus, as he does in the following sentence; in that case, this statement and the following polemical question are grossly misrepresenting Philoponus' view, because

is one and the same matter for all things, both celestial and sublunary, how could it be rational <to say> that the fifth body is matter for the things below the moon?[25]

(2) Next, either it is due to a superior and transcendent cause that the matter of the things in heaven does not accept a different form from the one it does have now; <in that case> it is not necessary that heaven be perishable on account of <its> matter;[26] or, as the <Grammarian> says in contradiction to himself, 'it will accept a different form at a different time'. In that case too it is not necessary that the heaven as a whole be perishable, but if at all only the parts, <which perish> because of the contraries changing into one another as they do in the case of the sublunary things. So if the matter <in heaven and below the moon> is one, this much befalls him simply because of his arguments: the things above appear to come to be below and what is here appears to come to be above, as it does to drunk people, so that the sun comes to be here by nature, a man in heaven, and the celestial things with the things here. But what would be more absurd than this?[27] Or if the matter of heaven, being one, is able to receive all of the forms there, it is either so capable to no purpose or even the things there change at some time into one another. Yet even so, his aim to show that the world is perishable will not come to pass. For it is not the case that something below the moon must at some time necessarily not be because its parts are changing into one another while they attach to the underlying matter. For here <below> the destruction of one thing is the generation of another; what contrivance could destroy a system like that? And so, how much better and more appropriate to the creator-god it would have been on the one hand to declare eternal the things immediately created by him who is in every respect always the same, changing neither substantially nor in potentiality

20

25

30

35

1331,1

in the passage he grants a fifth element merely for the sake of the argument. Philoponus in fact denies the existence of a fifth body and proposes that three-dimensional extension (on this see n. 29 below) be regarded as the substrate of both the celestial and sublunary regions.

[25] According to Aristotelian doctrine, only the four elements earth, air, fire and water are found below the moon.

[26] Because God can override its tendency to change forms.

[27] Curiously, this rhetorical question is omitted in both Marcianus 219 and the Aldine edition.

nor in actuality. That way we avoid his being at some time a world-creator, at another time left idle, unproductive and solitary. And <how much better> on the other hand <to say> that the sublunary <region>, which came to be through eternal and eternally moving things created by him, possesses
5   parts that come to be and pass away, in order that even the remotest thing of the world be generated through the creator's goodness. But he who exists always produced it, and it is eternal too because the destruction of one thing is the generation of another, since he has made generation perpetual.

> <The third of Philoponus' own arguments: At least the world is perishable so far as its nature is concerned, even if God can override the natural tendency to perish. First proof: The things in heaven are composite substances and therefore by definition subject to decomposition.>

In his third argument <the Grammarian> seems to follow Plato as he attempts to show that the things in heaven do not possess infinite capacity *in virtue of their own nature*, even
10   though they would not perish because they are held together by a capacity stronger than their[28] nature. 'For if, he says, the things in heaven are composite, and if composites can decompose by definition (*logon ekhei luseôs*), and if the things which can, by definition, decompose can be destroyed (because the decomposition of the elements is the destruction of the compound), and if that which can be destroyed does not possess an infinite capacity, then, *as far as depends on their own nature* the things in heaven do not possess an infinite
15   capacity.' We are informed shortly afterwards that he holds in agreement with Plato that the creator will not separate that which he has put together well, despite the fact that it can be destroyed. 'And, <the Grammarian> says, those who claim that heaven consists not of the four elements but of the fifth body, they too claim that it is composed of a substrate, the fifth body, and a form, <for example the form> of the sun or
20   the moon. And so, he says, if one took all the forms away, their

---

[28] Read *heautôn* at 1331,10 with MSS A and G.

three-dimensional <substrate>[29] alone would remain in virtue of which the celestial bodies would not differ in anything from the bodies familiar to us (*ta par' hêmin sômata*),[30] so that the things in heaven, being composites, can also decompose by definition and be destroyed. And because of this their capacity is not infinite, even though according to Plato they are never destroyed because they are held together by a bond which is stronger than their own nature, the will of   25 God.'

<Simplicius replies:>

(1) Now this argument makes it clear that because of his vanity he has forgotten his initial thesis.[31] For he set himself to demonstrate that heaven is generated and perishable, but now he shows it to possess a finite capacity and to be perishable because of its own nature, yet to remain together undissolved and imperishable because of the will of God.

(2) And quite clearly, God's will would not have offered such   30 a good to something which is not suitably disposed (*epitêdeiôs ekhon*) to accept it;[32] even if heaven does not possess the infinite kinetic capacity all at once because it is moved and

[29] *to trikhêi diastaton*. Philoponus arrived at this idea in his *Physics* commentary and esp. in the *contra Proclum* through a critique of the Aristotelian concept of 'prime matter' which Neoplatonists interpreted as both incorporeal and formless. Philoponus argued that this conception of matter must be false; the ultimate ontological substrate of the physical world cannot possibly be either: matter must be corporeal if it is to give substance to body, and, since matter never occurs without form, it must possess some kind of extension. He therefore abandoned the traditional concept altogether and preferred to speak of 'the three-dimensional' as fundamental, meaning 'corporeal extension in three dimensions'. The exact interpretation of this important aspect of Philoponus' ontology is controversial; for further and more detailed discussion see R. Sorabji, in *Philoponus and the Rejection of Aristotelian Science*, London and Ithaca N.Y. 1987, 18-23, C. Wildberg, *John Philoponus' Criticism of Aristotle's Theory of Aether*, Berlin and New York 1988, 204-21, and M. Wolff, *Fallgesetz und Massebegriff*, Berlin and New York 1971, 108ff.

[30] This of course would not have been accepted by his opponents.

[31] Simplicius' charge of forgetting is unfair. Philoponus is progressing, as we know from other texts, by meeting counterarguments. If his first arguments are met by the Platonic reply that God can override the world's natural tendency for dissolution, then he requires his opponents to distinguish 'perishable so far as depends on its nature' from plain 'perishable'. He also offers in other treatises an argument that even God cannot override the natural fact that the world has a beginning in time, see Sorabji, *Matter, Space and Motion*, ch. 15.

[32] This is an important idea in Simplicius: the world's nature is not simply overridden if it is preserved for ever by God, because it must be part of its nature to be able to receive this gift; cf. 1334, 24-6.

finite, it has nevertheless been naturally designed to be moved for ever.

(3) Unsound too is his assumption that the fifth body is a compound in the sense that it can decompose by definition.
35   For the term decomposition applies to those things which have a substrate that does not sustain the forms, and which have been put together by opposite forms that change into one another. But the things in heaven possess the form of circular motion (*to kuklophorêtikon eidos*) which has no contrary to it because no motion is contrary to circular motion, as Aristotle showed in the first <book> of *On the Heavens*.[33] To my mind I
1332,1   have demonstrated that when this man objected against these demonstrations he did not comprehend a thing of what Aristotle said.

<Philoponus, second proof: It can be shown that bodies, so far as their own nature is concerned, are perishable and (a necessary and perhaps sufficient condition) have a finite capacity. Proof by divisibility into units which are perishable and of finite capacity.[34]>

Next he attempts to show that both the totalities of the elements and the things in heaven have a finite capacity. Nothing, however, is absurd about that, given that they do not
·5   possess an infinite capacity all at once because they are finite <bodies>. Absolutely absurd, however, is the thought that what does not posssess an infinite capacity all at once is identical with what is perishable. He claims, then, that in the *Physics* lectures[35] it has been shown that no chance form, be it composite or simple, exists in a chance magnitude (for there would not be a man the size of a finger or a mosquito the size

---

[33] See *de Caelo* 1.4, 270b32-271a33; 270a12-22. Circularity, unlike hot, cold, fluid and dry, the qualities found in the other four elements, has no contrary. On Aristotle's peculiar reasoning see Wildberg, *John Philoponus' Criticism of Aristotle's Theory of Aether*, ch. 4.3.

[34] The connection of thought is obscured by Simplicius, who admits he is paraphrasing. The explicit references to perishability are at first ignored and only the references to finite capacity highlighted. The two are connected by the idea of 'insofar as its own nature is concerned', and by the fact that finite capacity is a necessary and sufficient condition of destructibility. This equivalence is only later brought out by Simplicius.

[35] cf. Aristotle *Physics* 1.4, 187b7-188a18.

of an arm).[36] Nor does water exist in a chance magnitude, but 10
whenever water is split up so many times that the magnitude
resulting from the division is smaller than the <magnitude>
which naturally receives the form of water, the water is
destroyed, for example, when after dipping the tip of our
finger into water we make the form of water disappear by
spreading the moisture, rubbing it down, and dividing it into
smallest parts (*brakhutata*).[37] 'On this ground, he says, it will 15
be shown that not even the totalities of the elements partake
of an infinite capacity. For we see that in as much as the
magnitude of the elements is diminished, so much the faster
they undergo destruction, in as much as it is increased, so
much the slower. Let it be supposed, then, that a cup of water
is capable of lasting for one year. Each quantity of water of the
same size will then hold out for the same time. But now, since 20
the mass of water as a whole is finite the whole mass will
evidently be measured out by the cup and the whole of water
will be divisible into a finite number of cups. But each of the
parts possesses a finite capacity; therefore, what is put
together by all these parts will have a finite capacity, which is
also true of the other <elements>. By these <arguments>, 25
he says, it has therefore been shown that each of the four
elements, taken as a whole, has by itself a finite capacity.'

<Simplicius replies:>

(1) This is what he has to say in almost his own words.[38] It
is perhaps first requisite to understand to what use he puts
the first assumption that a form, whatever it may be, does not
exist in a chance magnitude. For the hypothesis concerning 30
the cup of water did not require that if the water were divided
into cups each of which lasts for a year that the whole <of
water> last for a year too, since time is not put together by
divided cups. Let this be the statement against the rotten part
of the hypothesis.

(2) One should consider next that in supposing that the

---

[36] End of parenthesis after *genoito an* in line 1332,9.
[37] i.e. there could be smaller parts because of the infinite divisibility of body, but
they could not be *water*.
[38] A sign that Simplicius does not guarantee exact quotation.

whole of the water may perish in a finite time he has not reflected on the simultaneous change of the other elements
35   into water. But just as the perishing parts of water change into other elements, the parts of the other elements change likewise into water, and this <process> is perpetual and eternal because the destruction of one thing is the generation of another.

(3) Moreover, the cause of destruction and generation for the things here is above all the eternal motion along the
40   ecliptic circle; so how can the totalities of the elements possibly be destroyed?[39]

<Philoponus applies the divisibility argument to the heavens.>

But as if he has shown just that, <the Grammarian> brings
1333,1   up a forceful <argument>: 'We will show by the same argument that all things in heaven, too, are of finite capacity' – although he does not adduce the same argument. For he states that none of the celestial forms nor the whole world are naturally put together in a chance magnitude – an assumption which he had not used earlier. 'If then every body,
5   he says, is infinitely divisible, and if the things in heaven are bodies too, then they are no doubt infinitely divisible as well in virtue of their own definition (*tôi idiôi logôi*) (according to which they are extended things), even though they may never be divided, just as matter by its own definition is devoid of form even though it never occurs without form. And the three-dimensional[40] by its own definition is devoid of quality even though it never occurs without quality. But it is a form
10   supervening from outside which is the cause of not being divided or of being difficult to divide or even of being indivisible for us, as in the case of the diamond. If, then, the things in heaven, being bodies, are infinitely divisible because they are magnitudes, if someone divided them in thought (*tôi logôi*), just as we separate the forms from matter in thought, it

---

[39] The point is that their movement and change is eternal.
[40] cf. above n. 29.

is clear that the cutting will arrive at some particular magnitude in which their forms will not be able to exist. Concomitantly with such a division the forms will therefore 15
perish. Thus, if insofar as they are bodies they admit of division in virtue of the definition of their nature, and <so> admit of destruction (since our mind transposes into actuality the attributes that apply to them merely potentially), and if none of the things which are of the formal character to be destroyed (*ouden tôn logon ekhontôn phthoras*) has an infinite capacity by nature, none of the celestial bodies will consequently be in possession of an infinite capacity in virtue of its nature. For 20
that which has an infinite capacity by nature is not of the formal character to be destroyed, nor in the bare concept of it (*kata psilên epinoian*) would it be suspected of being destroyed any more than entities that are simple in every respect and separated from relation to bodies. For we are unable even to imagine in virtue of what definition in physics one could conceive of them as perishable. For our question at the moment is this: What is the natural definition of each thing? and not: What is added to something by the transcendent cause?[41] In 25
consequence, although one might agree that the heavens do not perish because they are held together by the will of God, it is emphatically not the case as well that in virtue of their own nature they will not accept the formal character of destruction.[42] But what is of the formal character to be destroyed is not infinite in capacity. For how could it be that this formal character (*logos*) of destruction which is comprehended by our mind will not at some time also become actual?[43] For the fact 30
that they remain and are not led to destruction now is no proof of them being imperishable by nature, as we have shown in the

---

[41] i.e. God.

[42] This is the concession Philoponus still wants; it is the main theme of the third of his own arguments. The statement that the celestial body does not possess infinite capacity is subordinate to this aim. Simplicius obscures this.

[43] The implication of this question is not entirely clear. It seems that all Philoponus claims, and ought to claim at this point, is that heaven is perishable, not that, of necessity, it will in fact perish at some time. Simplicius, at any rate, seems eager to foist the stronger claim on Philoponus, a position much easier to repudiate; cf. also below 1334,26-39.

fourth <book> of the *Contra Aristotelem.*'[44]

<Simplicius replies:>

(1) I have cited this in so many words with the intention both to expose to those who come across him the mental attitude (*hexis*) of this man and to make even more obvious
35   that he regards having a finite capacity as identical with being perishable,[45] whereby he does not even have the concept of that which has being ad infinitum.[46]

(2) Moreover, this man is clearly ignorant of the way in which every body is said to be infinitely divisible; it is a statement against those who claim that bodies are composed of atoms. It shows that every body is extended as well as segmented (*meriston*) and has parts and it, <the part>, is of
40   such <parts> and is not composed of atoms. Now, that which
1334,1 is infinitely divisible is not said to be divided throughout (*diairoumenon pantelôs*) and to lose its continuity. For then it would no longer be infinitely divisible; rather the thing in

---

[44] See esp. fr. 80 (= Simpl. *in Cael.* 142,7-25) in Wildberg, *Philoponus: Against Aristotle on the Eternity of the World,* 90f.: 'But, <the Grammarian> says, the fact that in the entire past the heavens do not seem to have changed either as a whole or in <their> parts must not be taken as a proof that they are completely indestructible and ungenerated. For there are also some animals which live longer than others, and <some> parts of the earth, mountains for example, and stones like the diamonds, exist almost as long as the whole of time, and there is no record that Mount Olympus had a beginning of existence, or <was subject to> increase or diminution. And in the case of mortal animals, for the time that they are to be preserved it is necessary that the most important of their parts retain their proper nature, so that as long as God wants the world to exist it is also necessary that the most important of its parts be preserved. But it has been agreed that the heavens as a whole as well as in <their> parts are the most important and most essential parts of the world. For by their movement all bodies inside are guided naturally. Therefore it is necessary that as long as the world is to be preserved, the heavens will not abandon their proper nature in any respect, neither as a whole nor in <their> parts. But if it has rightly been shown by Aristotle that all bodies have a limited capacity, and if the heavens, too, are a body, <then> it is evident that they are also liable to destruction because the term 'destruction' applies to them, even though so far they clearly have not been affected by anything leading to destruction.'

[45] So far Philoponus has only shown that the possession of a finite capacity is a necessary condition for perishability. Now Simplicius asserts that Philoponus wants it to be a sufficient condition also.

[46] A calumny. Again Simplicius ignores that what Philoponus is asking for is a recognition of the distinction between 'perishability by nature' and 'actual destruction'. At least the former must be conceded, he is saying. He recognises quite explicitly Plato's point that the world may be given perpetual existence by God. What may be true is that Philoponus does not distinguish the infinite capacity of the world to be moved and kept in existence as being a capacity ad infinitum.

question as a whole is divided into parts which are not
detached from one another but are divided and separated in
extension, but not in the sense of having been cut (*hôs
temnomena*) and torn apart from one another (*apospômenon
allêlôn*). For even if they are never torn apart, bodies are   5
nevertheless segmented (*memeristai*) in extension and are
divided (*diêirêtai*) into parts. For that which is as such
incorporeal fits as a whole to itself as a whole because it is
unextended and it is not divided into parts; but the body,
which extends <spatially>, is scattered in parts of which
different ones have come to be in different places, and it is
divided in this way. And the fact that bodies are infinitely
divisible is common to all bodies and belongs to them as   10
bodies. For even though it does not belong to the nature of my
right side to be at some time cut off from my left, the two sides
are nevertheless divided (*diêirêtai*) from one another and
marked off (*diôristai*) and are segmented in actuality
(*memeristai kat' energeian*). But it remains that bodies which
can suffer are of a nature to be cut (*temnesthai pephuken*) into
things which can be cut (*eis tmêta*) and are themselves bodies,
<bodies>, however, which cannot suffer are not cut, neither
in definition (*logôi*) nor in the thoughts of those who think   15
prudently; nevertheless, they are divided and segmented in
actuality, yet remain continuous in their corporeal
extension.[47]

(3) But since the <Grammarian> has heard, or rather
misheard, that every body is divisible, he mentally cut down
(*katetemen*) the things in heaven into smallest parts. Now this
is mad and mindless, but less so than to expect that this mind
of his leads to actuality as well.[48] For he says: 'The <things in   20
heaven> admit of destruction because our mind leads the
things that belong to them potentially into actuality.'[49] Now,
if the divisibility ad infinitum of bodies does not necessitate
that at some time the things in heaven are wholly cut down

---

[47] All bodies *qua* bodies are continuous and therefore divisible (*diaireton*) and
segmented (*meristhai*) into actual parts. But only bodies which are passive, i.e.
subject to external influences, may also be actually cut (*temnesthai*), whereas
impassive bodies cannot be so cut, not even in a thought experiment.

[48] Philoponus did not say leads to actuality, only to actuality in thought, i.e. we
think of it as actualised.

[49] cf. 1333,15-17.

into smallest parts, then it is also not necessary that they lose their form, neither through the will of God nor in virtue of their own nature. For the will of God supplies the goods not to

25 this and that at random but to those things that are suitably disposed.

(4) It is further worth objecting that he thinks that whatever he[50] can imagine can also come to be. He says: 'For we cannot even imagine destruction of the things which are not related to bodies and are imperishable by nature.'[51] And, according to *his* <kind of> conversion by negation,[52] <an

30 inference> which he does not master, he would say that the things of which we can imagine destruction are not imperishable by nature. This is the magnitude of the power which the <Grammarian> has assigned to his imagination. So why should one be surprised, if someone who can imagine heaven to be perishable contends straightway that it is really perishing, when indeed he has been afflicted by the same madness against God?[53] But since he does not understand how the speech (*logos*) on the dissolution of the heavens

35 uttered by Plato through the mouth of the demiurge is meant[54] but changes it into an argument on destruction and because of that imagines heaven to perish, he vigorously exclaims the following against heaven itself: 'From what source can it be, he asks, that this formal character (*logos*) of destruction which is apprehended by our minds will not at some time become actual?'[55]

(5) The fact that until now <heaven> has not suffered

40 anything comparable to what perishable things have suffered does not discountenance him in the least. But however much

1335,1 he wrote on the subject, as he claims, in the fourth <book> of the *Contra Aristotelem*, I have scrutinised it to the best of my ability when I commented on the first book of *On the*

---

[50] In 1334,26 I am inclined to read *houtos* with the Aldine edition, not *houtôs* with MS A.

[51] cf. 1333,21-3.

[52] The Stoic term for transposition: $(p \to q) \to (\sim p \to \sim q)$. Simplicius is highly critical of Philoponus' use of the inference, see Simpl. *in Cael.* 28,14-31,6. On the problem, see Wildberg, *John Philoponus' Criticism of Aristotle's Theory of Aether*, 113-17. It appears, however, as if Simplicius is foisting this inference on Philoponus at this point, accusing him of commiting the fallacy of denying the antecedent.

[53] A jibe at the doctrine of the death and resurrection of Christ.

[54] cf. Plato *Timaeus* 41a7-d3.

[55] cf. above 1333,28-30 and n. 43.

Heavens.[56] And now one must object to him that as regards those things that come to be and perish, the time past their prime until the end is either equal to or greater than the time from the beginning to the prime. Now heaven, as this man 5 believes, came to be 6,000 years ago or more and is already at the end of its days – a further idea which he is entirely pleased with –, why then did he not show us that <heaven> is past its prime, heading towards destruction? Yet, if nothing else, with regard to motion at any rate he ought to think that <heaven> is slower because it happens to be at the end of its years. And yet it does not make days, nights and hours longer now, as is 10 shown by the actions performed in them when compared to those of long ago, like tillage and journeys by land and sea. For the day's distance of a journey is the same even now, and oxen plough the same on one day or even less, and the buckets of water-clocks designed by the same methods transport in each hour the same amount of water in and out as before. 15

<The fourth of Philoponus' own arguments: The whole has finite capacity because the parts have, as is shown (a) by their dependence on the whole and (b) by the fact that they must be smaller than the whole.>

But one must proceed to the remaining and, as he claims, his fourth argument by means of which he intends to show that the capacity of the celestial body is not infinite. And it is true also according to Aristotle who denied any body an infinite 20 capacity which is all at once but assigned to the body which moves in a circle[57] motion and existence ad infinitum. But the <Grammarian>, who does away with infinite capacity as he does away with eternity, aims right away at putting perishability to the fore. He states, then, that if the celestial <body> were infinite in capacity, it would be necessary that each of its parts be either infinite or finite in capacity. 'But, he says, <the parts> do not possess an infinite <capacity> 25 because what possesses an infinite capacity is self-sufficient.

---

[56] cf. Simplicius *in Cael.* 119-42, where he is dealing with book 4 of Philoponus' *Contra Aristotelem*. On Philoponus' arguments and Simplicius' replies see Wildberg, *Philoponus: Against Aristotle on the Eternity of the World*, 77-91 and id., *John Philoponus' Criticism*, 187-204.

[57] i.e. the celestial body, on Aristotle's geocentric hypothesis.

But each of the parts of heaven needs each of the other parts and the whole in order to exist, if indeed parts <belong to the class> of relatives. For parts are <parts> of a whole, and they exchange their respective powers with one another, as the moon and the compound activity (*summiktos energeia*) of the things there towards the things here most clearly show. And so, he says, if the parts are not self- sufficient they do not have infinite capacity either.'

<Supporting argument:>

30   He thinks to show this in a different way too: 'If the capacity of each part is infinite, the whole, he claims, will possess either the same capacity as each of its parts or a larger one. Yet if it is larger there will be something larger than infinity, which is impossible; on the other alternative the same part will turn out to be both infinite and finite – infinite by hypothesis, finite
35   insofar as it is exceeded by something. But it is in fact impossible that the capacity of the whole and the part be equal. For we clearly see everywhere that the whole possesses a larger capacity than each of its parts. For even though the cold quality in a part of water is the same as in the whole, the capacity which holds the being of the water together (*hê sunektikê tou einai dunamis*)[58] is not the same. Rather, the larger the parts are that bodies consist of, the longer they last.
40   And so, if the capacity of each of the parts is not infinite, it is
1336,1 finite. In consequence, the whole is finite as well, for it is impossible that something put together both in number and in capacity (*kai arithmôi kai dunamei*) from finite parts be infinite in capacity. It remains, therefore, he claims, that heaven as a whole as well as each of its parts is finite in capacity. All things below the moon are of this sort.'

<Simplicius replies:>

5   (1) And against this the same things have to be remarked briefly that neither the moving whole nor its parts can have all at once the infinite capacity to cause motion which

---

[58] Cf. *SVF* 2, 439f. Philoponus uses Stoic terminology and ideas. As Galen reports, the Stoics spoke of *sunektikê dunamis* as the cause of the maintenance of things. Fire,

Aristotle attributes to the prime and eternal mover. But <whole and parts> do possess an infinite capacity to be moved and to be generated, though not all at once. For both motion and generation have their being in <a chain of> 10 generation, but ad infinitum. In this way infinity belongs equally to the whole and to the parts, given the fact that neither can the whole exist without the parts nor the parts without the whole. For we see, too, in the case of things which last for a certain time, for example animals, that necessarily the being of the parts and of the whole have the same duration; however, in virtue of their own substance (*ousian*), 15 i.e. if not considered as parts, some exist for a longer time than the whole, as for example the parts[59] of the whole of animals. For although the whole has perished the bones remain. Hence, it is not true that the continuance (*paratasis*)[60] of being in the whole derives from each of the parts and from the capacity in each part, in such a way that the parts, when put together, thereby bestow a many times larger capacity of being on the whole, as if the whole remained 20 in being many times longer – especially <not> in the case where the whole consists of always the same parts. For it is unsurprising if the whole of water and each of the elements remains in being for a longer time than its parts since it embraces different parts at different times as some parts come to be and others perish. However, not even this man would say that the totality of heaven, which always enjoys the 25 same parts, should last for a longer time than its parts. Being then is in both cases, for the whole and for the parts, equally being ad infinitum and does not differ in temporal continuance (if indeed, as even this <Grammarian> concedes, parts and whole necessarily exist together as relatives), but it differs in the greater comprehensiveness of being and perhaps of temporal duration. For the time of more 30 general things is more general, not in the sense of continuing

air and *pneuma* were capable of keeping themselves in being, whereas water and earth relied on some other *sunektikê aitia* to sustain them. In the *de Anima*, Aristotle spoke of the soul as the cause which keeps opposite bodies like fire and earth together, 2.4, 416a6-9; cf. 1.5, 411b8.

[59] The editor's proposed<*osta*> in line 1336,16 is not necessary.

[60] On this term's career first in Stoic grammar and later in Neoplatonic philosophy (e.g. Damascius and Simplicius, who defined time as the measure of the continuance of being) see P. Hoffmann, 'Paratasis', *Revue des Études Grecques* 96 (1983), 1-26.

for more years, but in the sense that it embraces within itself the times of more particular things, just as the being of the parts is embraced in the being of the whole. But let the <Grammarian> finally be left alone since he has met with an examination sufficient, I think, for the immediate purposes in hand.

English-Greek Glossary

above: *anô*
absurd: *atopos*
accept (see also admit): *epidekhesthai, katadekhesthai*
active: *energêtikos*
activity: *energeia*
actuality: *energeia*
ad infinitum: *ep' apeiron*
add: *prostithenai*
adduce (see also conclude): *epagein*
admit (see also accept): *epidekhesthai*
agree (see also concede): *sunkhôrein*
animal: *zôion*
apprehend: *katalambanein*
arbitration: *diaita*
argument: *epikheirêma, epikheirêsis, logos*
atom: *atomon*
attempt (v): *epiballesthai, epikheirein, peirasthai*
attitude: *hexis*

beginning: *arkhê*
belong to: *huparkhein*
below: *katô*
body: *sôma*
bond: *desmos*
bone: *osteon*
book: *biblion*

capacity (see also potential): *dunamis*
cause: *aitia*
celestial body (see also heaven): *ouranion sôma*
change (n): *metabolê*
change (v): *metaballein*
circle: *kuklos*
cite: *paratithenai*
come to be: *gignesthai*
comment (n): *hupomnêma*

commentator: *exêgêtês*
composite: *summiktos, sunthetos*
compound: *suntheton*
concede (see also agree): *homologein, sunkhôrein*
conceive: *epinoein*
concept (see also mind, conception): *ennoia, epinoia*
conception: *ennoia*
conclude (see also adduce): *epagein*
continuance: *paratasis*
continue: *parateinein*
continuity: *sunekheia*
continuous: *sunekhês*
contrary: *enantion*
contrivance: *mêkhanê*
conversion by negation: *sun antithesei antistrophê*
creator (see also divine craftsman): *dêmiourgos, kosmopoios*
cut (n): *tomê*
cut (v): *apotemnein, temnein*

dare: *tolman*
decomposition (see also dissolution): *dialusis, lusis*
definition (see also argument, formal character): *logos*
demonstrate: *apodeiknunai*
demonstration (see also proof): *apodeixis*
deny: *apophanai*
destruction: *phthora*
detached: *apespasmenos*
diamond: *adamas*
differ: *diapherein*
difference: *diaphora*
diminish: *meioun*
discountenance: *dusôpein*
disparage: *kataphronein*
dissolution (see also decomposition): *lusis*
distance: *diastêma*
distinguish: *diorizein*
divide: *diairein*
divided: *diairoumenos, diêirêmenos*
divine craftsman (see also creator): *dêmiourgos*
divisible: *diairetos*
division: *diairesis*

ecliptic circle: *loxos kuklos*
element: *stoikheion*
encounter (v): *entunkhanein*
end: *teleutê, telos*
eternal: *aïdios*

eternity: *aïdiotês*
examination: *exetasis*
exchange: *metadidonai*
exist: *huphistanai*
extended: *diastatos*
extension: *diastasis*

fifth body (aether): *pempton sôma*
finite: *peperasmenos*
fit (v): *epharmottein*
follow: *hepesthai, parakolouthein*
forget: *epilanthanein*
form: *eidos*
formal character (see also argument, definition): *logos*
formless: *aneideos*

generated: *genêtos*
generation: *genesis*
god: *theos*
goodness: *agathotês*
grasp: *katamathein*

heaven (see also celestial body): *ouranos*
help (v): *suntelein*
holding together: *sunektikos*
hypothesis: *hupothesis*

idle: *argos*
imagination: *phantasia*
imagine: *phantazein*
immediate: *prosekhês*
imperishable: *aphthartos*
impossible: *adunatos*
incongruity: *apemphainon*
incorporeal: *asômatos*
increase: *parauxein*
indivisible: *adiairetos*
infer: *sunagein*
inference: *sunagôgê*
infinite: *apeiros*
infinity: *apeiria*
inherence: *hupoikouria*
intention (see also purpose): *skopos*
interpret: *saphênizein*

last, remain: *arkein, diarkein*
layman: *idiôtês*

lecture: *skholê*
lose: *apoballein*

mad: *manikos*
madness: *paranoia*
magnitude: *megethos*
mass: *onkos*
matter: *hulê*
method: *methodos*
mind (see also concept): *epinoia*
mindless: *paraphrôn*
misconception: *paranoia*
moisture: *ikmas*
moon: *selênê*
motion: *kinêsis*
move: *kinein*

natural: *phusikos*
nature: *phusis*
necessary: *anankê, anankaios*
need (v): *deisthai*
number: *arithmos*

object (v): *antilegein, hupantan*
obvious: *phaneros*
occur: *sumbainein*
oppose: *enistanai*
opposite: *antikeimenos*

part: *meros, morion*
particular: *merikos*
pass away: *phtheiresthai*
passive: *pathêtikos*
pause: *paula*
perish: *apollusthai*
perishable: *phthartos*
perpetual: *endelekhês*
piety: *theosebeia*
possess: *ekhein*
possible: *dunatos*
potential (see also capacity): *to dunamei*
powerful: *dunamikos*
prevent: *kôluein*
prime matter: *prôtê hulê*
prime: *akmê*
produce: *mêkhanasthai*
proof (see also demonstration): *apodeixis*

purpose (see also intention): *skopos*
put together: *harmottein, suntithenai*

quality: *poiotês*

realise: *ennoiein*
receive: *dekhesthai*
refute: *elenkhein*
relation: *skhesis*
relative (n): *to pros ti*
remain: *kataleipein, leipesthai*
remarkable: *thaumastos*
reside in: *enuparkhein*
rotten: *sathros*

scatter: *diarriptein*
segmented: *meristos*
self-substantial: *authupostatos*
self-sufficient: *autarkês*
separate (v): *khôrizein*
separated: *kekhôrismenos*
show: *deiknunai, endidonai*
simple: *haplos*
solitary: *erêmos*
sphere: *sphaira*
split (v): *katatemnein*
star: *astêr*
sublunary bodies/things: *ta hupo selênên*
substance: *ousia*
substrate: *hupokeimenon*
suffer: *paskhein*
suffice: *arkein*
suitable: *epitêdeios*
sun: *hêlios*
supplier: *khorêgos*
supply: *khorêgein*
suspect: *hupotopein*
sustain: *stegein*
system: *sustêma*

tear apart: *apospasthai*
thesis: *prothesis*
think: *noein, nomizein*
three-dimensional: *trikhêi diastaton*
time: *khronos*
totality: *holotês*
transcendent: *exêirêmenos*

Greek-English Index

References are to the page and line numbers in the margin of the translation.

Subject Index

References are to the page and line numbers in the margins of the translation.

activity, actuality, 1327,31; 1328,36; 1329,32; 1331,1; 1333,17.30; 1334,12- 39; 1335,29

animal, 1336,13.16

atom, 1333,38

body: can be moved forever, 1328,22-39
    fifth body (aether), 1330,10-21; 1331,18.34
    finite body cannot be moved forever, 1328,9
    finite body possesses finite capacity, 1327,13.27; 1328,8.35; 1329,14; 1335,20
    infinitely divisible, 1333,5-20; 1333,36-1334,18
sublunary bodies, 1330,24-1331,7

capacity: active, 1327,33f.
    finite in a finite body, 1327,13.39; 1328,1
    infinite, 1327,24.38; 1328,17-30
    passive, 1327,34
    resides in a body, 1327,29
    used homonymously according to Alexander, 1327,37

celestial body, see heaven

change, 1328,32; 1332,35

conversion by negation, 1334,29

creator, see god

decomposition, 1331,35

destruction, 1330,36; 1331,7-23; 1332,17.38; 1333,18-30; 1334,20-38; 1335,8

diamond, 1333,11

dissolution, see decomposition

distance, 1335,13

division, 1328,17; 1333,15f.

ecliptic circle, 1332,39

element: change of elements into one another, 1330,4; 1330,34-1331,7; 1332,34; 1336,22
    their totalities have finite capacity, 1332,3-26

eternity, rejected by Philoponus, 1327,6

form: compound of form and matter perishable, 1329,37
    does not exist in a chance magnitude, 1332,7-27; 1333,3
    of heaven, 1329,21
    separable from matter in thought, 1333,13

generation, infinite, 1328,16; 1336,9

god, demiurge, 1330,37-1331,7; 1331,15
    disparaged by Philoponus, 1327,2; 1334,33
    in Plato, 1334,34
    his will, 1331,25.29f.; 1333,26; 1334,24f.

goodness, of god, 1331,6

heaven: capable of infinite motion, 1329,1; 1331,33; 1335,20
    composite, 1331,10-25
    consists of matter and form, 1329,20-24; 1330,7-17; 1331,17-20
    disparaged by Philoponus, 1327,1
    eternal, 1329,4
    fifth body, 1331,18
    finite with finite capacity, 1327,14; 1329,2-23; 1331,10-25; 1333,1-32; 1335,18-1336,5
    immutable, 1334,39-1335,16

140

Appendix
The Commentators*

The 15,000 pages of the Ancient Greek Commentaries on Aristotle are the largest corpus of Ancient Greek philosophy that has not been translated into English or other modern European languages. The standard edition (*Commentaria in Aristotelem Graeca, or CAG*) was produced by Hermann Diels as general editor under the auspices of the Prussian Academy in Berlin. Arrangements have now been made to translate at least a large proportion of this corpus, along with some other Greek and Latin commentaries not included in the Berlin edition, and some closely related non-commentary works by the commentators.

The works are not just commentaries on Aristotle, although they are invaluable in that capacity too. One of the ways of doing philosophy between A.D. 200 and 600, when the most important items were produced, was by writing commentaries. The works therefore represent the thought of the Peripatetic and Neoplatonist schools, as well as expounding Aristotle. Furthermore, they embed fragments from all periods of Ancient Greek philosophical thought: this is how many of the Presocratic fragments were assembled, for example. Thus they provide a panorama of every period of Ancient Greek philosophy.

The philosophy of the period from A.D. 200 to 600 has not yet been intensively explored by philosophers in English-speaking countries, yet it is full of interest for physics, metaphysics, logic, psychology, ethics and religion. The contrast with the study of the Presocratics is striking. Initially the incomplete Presocratic fragments might well have seemed less promising, but their interest is now widely known, thanks to the philological and philosophical effort that has been concentrated upon them. The incomparably vaster corpus which preserved so many of those fragments offers at least as much interest, but is still relatively little known.

The commentaries represent a missing link in the history of philosophy: the Latin-speaking Middle Ages obtained their

* Reprinted from the Editor's General Introduction to the series in Christian Wildberg, *Philoponus Against Aristotle on the Eternity of the World*, London and Ithaca N.Y., 1987.

knowledge of Aristotle at least partly through the medium of the commentaries. Without an appreciation of this, mediaeval interpretations of Aristotle will not be understood. Again, the ancient commentaries are the unsuspected source of ideas which have been thought, wrongly, to originate in the later mediaeval period. It has been supposed, for example, that Bonaventure in the thirteenth century invented the ingenious arguments based on the concept of infinity which attempt to prove the Christian view that the universe had a beginning. In fact, Bonaventure is merely repeating arguments devised by the commentator Philoponus 700 years earlier and preserved in the meantime by the Arabs. Bonaventure even uses Philoponus' original examples. Again, the introduction of impetus theory into dynamics, which has been called a scientific revolution, has been held to be an independent invention of the Latin West, even if it was earlier discovered by the Arabs or their predecessors. But recent work has traced a plausible route by which it could have passed from Philoponus, via the Arabs, to the West.

The new availability of the commentaries in the sixteenth century, thanks to printing and to fresh Latin translations, helped to fuel the Renaissance break from Aristotelian science. For the commentators record not only Aristotle's theories, but also rival ones, while Philoponus as a Christian devises rival theories of his own and accordingly is mentioned in Galileo's early works more frequently than Plato.[1]

It is not only for their philosophy that the works are of interest. Historians will find information about the history of schools, their methods of teaching and writing and the practices of an oral tradition.[2] Linguists will find the indexes and translations an aid for studying the development of word meanings, almost wholly

---

[1] See Fritz Zimmermann, 'Philoponus' impetus theory in the Arabic tradition'; Charles Schmitt, 'Philoponus' commentary on Aristotle's *Physics* in the sixteenth century', and Richard Sorabji, 'John Philoponus', in Richard Sorabji (ed.), *Philoponus and the Rejection of Aristotelian Science* (London and Ithaca, N.Y. 1987).

[2] See e.g. Karl Praechter, 'Die griechischen Aristoteleskommentare', *Byzantinische Zeitschrift* 18 (1909), 516-38; M. Plezia, *de Commentariis Isagogicis* (Cracow 1947); M. Richard, 'Apo Phônês', *Byzantion* 20 (1950), 191-222; É. Evrard, *L'Ecole d'Olympiodore et la composition du commentaire à la physique de Jean Philopon*, Diss. (Liège 1957); L.G. Westerink, *Anonymous Prolegomena to Platonic Philosophy* (Amsterdam 1962) (new revised edition, translated into French, Collection Budé, forthcoming); A.-J. Festugière, 'Modes de composition des commentaires de Proclus', *Museum Helveticum* 20 (1963), 77-100, repr. in his *Études* (1971), 551-74; P. Hadot, 'Les divisions des parties de la philosophie dans l'antiquité', *Museum Helveticum* 36 (1979), 201-23; I. Hadot, 'La division néoplatonicienne des écrits d'Aristote', in J. Wiesner (ed.), *Aristoteles Werk und Wirkung* (Paul Moraux gewidmet), vol. 2 (Berlin 1986); I. Hadot, 'Les introductions aux commentaires exégétiques chez les auteurs néoplatoniciens et les auteurs chrétiens', in M. Tardieu (ed.), *Les règles de l'interprétation* (Paris 1987), 99-119. These topics will be treated, and a bibliography supplied, in a collection of articles on the commentators in general.

uncharted in Liddell and Scott's *Lexicon*, and for checking shifts in grammatical usage.

Given the wide range of interests to which the volumes will appeal, the aim is to produce readable translations, and to avoid so far as possible presupposing any knowledge of Greek. Footnotes will explain points of meaning, give cross-references to other works, and suggest alternative interpretations of the text where the translator does not have a clear preference. The introduction to each volume will include an explanation why the work was chosen for translation: none will be chosen simply because it is there. Two of the Greek texts are currently being re-edited – those of Simplicius *in Physica* and *in de Caelo* – and new readings will be exploited by translators as they become available. Each volume will also contain a list of proposed emendations to the standard text. Indexes will be of more uniform extent as between volumes than is the case with the Berlin edition, and there will be three of them: an English-Greek glossary, a Greek-English index, and a subject index.

The commentaries fall into three main groups. The first group is by authors in the Aristotelian tradition up to the fourth century A.D. This includes the earliest extant commentary, that by Aspasius in the first half of the second century A.D. on the *Nicomachean Ethics*. The anonymous commentary on Books 2, 3, 4 and 5 of the *Nicomachean Ethics*, in *CAG* vol. 20, is derived from Adrastus, a generation later.[3] The commentaries by Alexander of Aphrodisias (appointed to his chair between A.D. 198 and 209) represent the fullest flowering of the Aristotelian tradition. To his successors Alexander was The Commentator *par excellence*. To give but one example (not from a commentary) of his skill at defending and elaborating Aristotle's views, one might refer to his defence of Aristotle's claim that space is finite against the objection that an edge of space is conceptually problematic.[4] Themistius (*fl.* late 340s to 384 or 385) saw himself as the inventor of paraphrase, wrongly thinking that the job of commentary was completed.[5] In fact, the Neoplatonists were to introduce new dimensions into commentary. Themistius' own relation to the Neoplatonist as opposed to the Aristotelian tradition is a matter of controversy,[6] but it would be

[3] Anthony Kenny, *The Aristotelian Ethics* (Oxford 1978), 37, n.3; Paul Moraux, *Der Aristotelismus bei den Griechen*, vol. 2 (Berlin 1984), 323-30.

[4] Alexander, *Quaestiones* 3.12, discussed in my *Matter, Space and Motion* (London and Ithaca, N.Y. 1988). For Alexander see R.W. Sharples, 'Alexander of Aphrodisias: scholasticism and innovation', in W. Haase (ed.), *Aufstieg und Niedergang der römischen Welt*, part 2 *Principat*, vol. 36.2, *Philosophie und Wissenschaften* (1987).

[5] Themistius *in An. Post.* 1,2-12. See H.J. Blumenthal, 'Photius on Themistius (Cod.74): did Themistius write commentaries on Aristotle?', *Hermes* 107 (1979), 168-82.

[6] For different views, see H.J. Blumenthal, 'Themistius, the last Peripatetic commentator on Aristotle?', in Glen W. Bowersock, Walter Burkert, Michael C.J. Putnam, *Arktouros*, Hellenic Studies Presented to Bernard M.W. Knox (Berlin and

agreed that his commentaries show far less bias than the full-blown Neoplatonist ones. They are also far more informative than the designation 'paraphrase' might suggest, and it has been estimated that Philoponus' *Physics* commentary draws silently on Themistius six hundred times.[7] The pseudo-Alexandrian commentary on *Metaphysics* 6–14, of unknown authorship, has been placed by some in the same group of commentaries as being earlier than the fifth century.[8]

By far the largest group of extant commentaries is that of the Neoplatonists up to the sixth century A.D. Nearly all the major Neoplatonists, apart from Plotinus (the founder of Neoplatonism), wrote commentaries on Aristotle, although those of Iamblichus (c. 250 – c. 325) survive only in fragments, and those of three Athenians, Plutarchus (died 432), his pupil Proclus (410 – 485) and the Athenian Damascius (c. 462 – after 538), are lost.[9] As a result of these losses, most of the extant Neoplatonist commentaries come from the late fifth and the sixth centuries and a good proportion from Alexandria. There are commentaries by Plotinus' disciple and editor Porphyry (232 – 309), by Iamblichus' pupil Dexippus (c. 330), by Proclus' teacher Syrianus (died c. 437), by Proclus' pupil Ammonius (435/445 – 517/526), by Ammonius' three pupils Philoponus (c. 490 to 570s), Simplicius (wrote after 532, probably after 538) and Asclepius (sixth century), by Ammonius' next but one successor Olympiodorus (495/505 – after 565), by Elias (*fl.* 541?), by David (second half of the sixth century, or beginning of the seventh) and by Stephanus (took the chair in Constantinople c. 610). Further,

---

N.Y., 1979), 391-400; E.P. Mahoney, 'Themistius and the agent intellect in James of Viterbo and other thirteenth-century philosophers: (Saint Thomas Aquinas, Siger of Brabant and Henry Bate)', *Augustiniana* 23 (1973), 422-67, at 428-31; id., 'Neoplatonism, the Greek commentators and Renaissance Aristotelianism', in D.J. O'Meara (ed.), *Neoplatonism and Christian Thought* (Albany N.Y. 1982), 169-77 and 264-82, esp. n. 1, 264-6; Robert Todd, introduction to translation of Themistius *in DA 3,4-8*, forthcoming in a collection of translations by Frederick Schroeder and Robert Todd of material in the commentators relating to the intellect.

[7] H. Vitelli, *CAG* 17, p. 992, s.v. Themistius.

[8] The similarities to Syrianus (died c.437) have suggested to some that it predates Syrianus (most recently Leonardo Tarán, review of Paul Moraux, *Der Aristotelismus*, vol. 1, in *Gnomon* 46 (1981), 721-50 at 750), to others that it draws on him (most recently P. Thillet, in the Budé edition of Alexander *de Fato*, p. lvii). Praechter ascribed it to Michael of Ephesus (eleventh or twelfth century), in his review of *CAG* 22.2, in *Göttingische Gelehrte Anzeiger* 168 (1906), 861-907.

[9] The Iamblichus fragments are collected in Greek by Bent Dalsgaard Larsen, *Jamblique de Chalcis, Exégète et Philosophe* (Aarhus 1972), vol.2. Most are taken from Simplicius, and will accordingly be translated in due course. The evidence on Damascius' commentaries is given in L.G. Westerink, *The Greek Commentaries on Plato's Phaedo*, vol.2., Damascius (Amsterdam 1977), 11-12; on Proclus' in L.G. Westerink, *Anonymous Prolegomena to Platonic Philosophy* (Amsterdam 1962), xii, n.22; on Plutarchus' in H.M. Blumenthal, 'Neoplatonic elements in the de Anima commentaries', *Phronesis* 21 (1976), 75.

a commentary on the *Nicomachean Ethics* has been ascribed to Heliodorus of Prusa, an unknown pre-fourteenth-century figure, and there is a commentary by Simplicius' colleague Priscian of Lydia on Aristotle's successor Theophrastus. Of these commentators some of the last were Christians (Philoponus, Elias, David and Stephanus), but they were Christians writing in the Neoplatonist tradition, as was also Boethius who produced a number of commentaries in Latin before his death in 525 or 526.

The third group comes from a much later period in Byzantium. The Berlin edition includes only three out of more than a dozen commentators described in Hunger's *Byzantinisches Handbuch*.[10] The two most important are Eustratius (1050/1060 – c. 1120), and Michael of Ephesus. It has been suggested that these two belong to a circle organised by the princess Anna Comnena in the twelfth century, and accordingly the completion of Michael's commentaries has been redated from 1040 to 1138.[11] His commentaries include areas where gaps had been left. Not all of these gap-fillers are extant, but we have commentaries on the neglected biological works, on the *Sophistici Elenchi*, and a small fragment of one on the *Politics*. The lost *Rhetoric* commentary had a few antecedents, but the *Rhetoric* too had been comparatively neglected. Another product of this period may have been the composite commentary on the *Nicomachean Ethics* (*CAG* 20) by various hands, including Eustratius and Michael, along with some earlier commentators, and an improvisation for Book 7. Whereas Michael follows Alexander and the conventional Aristotelian tradition, Eustratius' commentary introduces Platonist, Christian and anti-Islamic elements.[12]

The composite commentary was to be translated into Latin in the next century by Robert Grosseteste in England. But Latin translations of various logical commentaries were made from the Greek still earlier by James of Venice (*fl. c.* 1130), a contemporary of Michael of Ephesus, who may have known him in Constantinople.

---

[10] Herbert Hunger, *Die hochsprachliche profane Literatur der Byzantiner*, vol.1 (= *Byzantinisches Handbuch*, part 5, vol.1) (Munich 1978), 25-41. See also B.N. Tatakis, *La Philosophie Byzantine* (Paris 1949).

[11] R. Browning, 'An unpublished funeral oration on Anna Comnena', *Proceedings of the Cambridge Philological Society* n.s. 8 (1962), 1-12, esp. 6-7.

[12] R. Browning, op. cit. H.D.P. Mercken, *The Greek Commentaries of the Nicomachean Ethics of Aristotle in the Latin Translation of Grosseteste, Corpus Latinum Commentariorum in Aristotelem Graecorum* VI 1 (Leiden 1973), ch.1, 'The compilation of Greek commentaries on Aristotle's Nicomachean Ethics'. Sten Ebbesen, 'Anonymi Aurelianensis I Commentarium in *Sophisticos Elenchos*', *Cahiers de l'Institut Moyen Age Grecque et Latin* 34 (1979), 'Boethius, Jacobus Veneticus, Michael Ephesius and "Alexander" ', pp. v-xiii; id., *Commentators and Commentaries on Aristotle's Sophistici Elenchi*, 3 parts, *Corpus Latinum Commentariorum in Aristotelem Graecorum*, vol. 7 (Leiden 1981); A. Preus, *Aristotle and Michael of Ephesus on the Movement and Progression of Animals* (Hildesheim 1981), introduction.

And later in that century other commentaries and works by commentators were being translated from Arabic versions by Gerard of Cremona (died 1187).[13] So the twelfth century resumed the transmission which had been interrupted at Boethius' death in the sixth century.

The Neoplatonist commentaries of the main group were initiated by Porphyry. His master Plotinus had discussed Aristotle, but in a very independent way, devoting three whole treatises (*Enneads* 6.1–3) to attacking Aristotle's classification of the things in the universe into categories. These categories took no account of Plato's world of Ideas, were inferior to Plato's classifications in the *Sophist* and could anyhow be collapsed, some of them into others. Porphyry replied that Aristotle's categories could apply perfectly well to the world of intelligibles and he took them as in general defensible.[14] He wrote two commentaries on the *Categories*, one lost, and an introduction to it, the *Isagôgê*, as well as commentaries, now lost, on a number of other Aristotelian works. This proved decisive in making Aristotle a necessary subject for Neoplatonist lectures and commentary. Proclus, who was an exceptionally quick student, is said to have taken two years over his Aristotle studies, which were called the Lesser Mysteries, and which preceded the Greater Mysteries of Plato.[15] By the time of Ammonius, the commentaries reflect a teaching curriculum which begins with Porphyry's *Isagôgê* and Aristotle's *Categories*, and is explicitly said to have as its final goal a (mystical) ascent to the supreme Neoplatonist deity, the One.[16] The curriculum would have progressed from Aristotle to Plato, and would have culminated in Plato's *Timaeus* and *Parmenides*. The latter was read as being about the One, and both works were established in this place in the curriculum at least by

[13] For Grosseteste, see Mercken as in n. 12. For James of Venice, see Ebbesen as in n. 12, and L. Minio-Paluello, 'Jacobus Veneticus Grecus', *Traditio* 8 (1952), 265-304; id., 'Giacomo Veneto e l'Aristotelismo Latino', in Pertusi (ed.), *Venezia e l'Oriente fra tardo Medioevo e Rinascimento* (Florence 1966), 53-74, both reprinted in his *Opuscula* (1972). For Gerard of Cremona, see M. Steinschneider, *Die europäischen Übersetzungen aus dem arabischen bis Mitte des 17. Jahrhunderts* (repr. Graz 1956); E. Gilson, *History of Christian Philosophy in the Middle Ages* (London 1955), 235-6 and more generally 181-246. For the translators in general, see Bernard G. Dod, 'Aristoteles Latinus', in N. Kretzmann, A. Kenny, J. Pinborg (eds). *The Cambridge History of Latin Medieval Philosophy* (Cambridge 1982).

[14] See P. Hadot, 'L'harmonie des philosophies de Plotin et d'Aristote selon Porphyre dans le commentaire de Dexippe sur les Catégories', in *Plotino e il neoplatonismo in Oriente e in Occidente* (Rome 1974), 31-47; A.C. Lloyd, 'Neoplatonic logic and Aristotelian logic', *Phronesis* 1 (1955-6), 58-79 and 146-60.

[15] Marinus, *Life of Proclus* ch.13, 157,41 (Boissonade).

[16] The introductions to the *Isagôgê* by Ammonius, Elias and David, and to the *Categories* by Ammonius, Simplicius, Philoponus, Olympiodorus and Elias are discussed by L.G. Westerink, *Anonymous Prolegomena* and I. Hadot, 'Les Introductions', see n. 2. above.

the time of Iamblichus, if not earlier.[17]

Before Porphyry, it had been undecided how far a Platonist should accept Aristotle's scheme of categories. But now the proposition began to gain force that there was a harmony between Plato and Aristotle on most things.[18] Not for the only time in the history of philosophy, a perfectly crazy proposition proved philosophically fruitful. The views of Plato and of Aristotle had both to be transmuted into a new Neoplatonist philosophy in order to exhibit the supposed harmony. Iamblichus denied that Aristotle contradicted Plato on the theory of Ideas.[19] This was too much for Syrianus and his pupil Proclus. While accepting harmony in many areas,[20] they could see that there was disagreement on this issue and also on the issue of whether God was causally responsible for the existence of the ordered physical cosmos, which Aristotle denied. But even on these issues, Proclus' pupil Ammonius was to claim harmony, and, though the debate was not clear cut,[21] his claim was on the whole to prevail. Aristotle, he maintained, accepted Plato's Ideas,[22] at least in the form of principles (*logoi*) in the divine intellect, and these principles were in turn causally responsible for the beginningless existence of the physical universe. Ammonius wrote a whole book to show that Aristotle's God was thus an efficient cause, and though the book is lost, some of its principal arguments are preserved by Simplicius.[23] This tradition helped to make it possible for Aquinas to claim Aristotle's God as a Creator, albeit not in the sense of giving

[17] Proclus *in Alcibiadem 1* p.11 (Creuzer); Westerink, *Anonymous Prolegomena*, ch. 26, 12f. For the Neoplatonist curriculum see Westerink, Festugière, P. Hadot and I. Hadot in n. 2.

[18] See e.g. P. Hadot (1974), as in n. 14 above; H.J. Blumenthal, 'Neoplatonic elements in the de Anima commentaries', *Phronesis* 21 (1976), 64-87; H.A. Davidson, 'The principle that a finite body can contain only finite power', in S. Stein and R. Loewe (eds), *Studies in Jewish Religious and Intellectual History presented to A. Altmann* (Alabama 1979), 75-92; Carlos Steel, 'Proclus et Aristote', Proceedings of the Congrès Proclus held in Paris 1985, J. Pépin and H.D. Saffrey (eds), *Proclus, lecteur et interprète des anciens* (Paris 1987), 213-25; Koenraad Verrycken, *God en Wereld in de Wijsbegeerte van Ioannes Philoponus*, Ph.D. Diss. (Louvain 1985).

[19] Iamblichus ap. Elian *in Cat.* 123,1-3.

[20] Syrianus *in Metaph.* 80,4-7; Proclus *in Tim.* 1.6,21-7,16.

[21] Asclepius sometimes accepts Syranius' interpretation (*in Metaph.* 433,9-436,6); which is, however, qualified, since Syrianus thinks Aristotle is really committed willy-nilly to much of Plato's view (*in Metaph.* 117,25-118,11; ap. Asclepium *in Metaph.* 433,16; 450,22); Philoponus repents of his early claim that Plato is not the target of Aristotle's attack, and accepts that Plato is rightly attacked for treating ideas as independent entities outside the divine Intellect (*in DA* 37,18-31; *in Phys.* 225,4-226,11; *contra Procl.* 26,24-32,13; *in An. Post.* 242,14–243,25).

[22] Asclepius *in Metaph* from the voice of (i.e. from the lectures of) Ammonius 69,17-21; 71,28; cf. Zacharias *Ammonius, Patrologia Graeca* vol. 85, col. 952 (Colonna).

[23] Simplicius *in Phys.* 1361,11-1363,12. See H.A. Davidson; Carlos Steel; Koenraad Verrycken in n.18 above.

the universe a beginning, but in the sense of being causally responsible for its beginningless existence.[24] Thus what started as a desire to harmonise Aristotle with Plato finished by making Aristotle safe for Christianity. In Simplicius, who goes further than anyone,[25] it is a formally stated duty of the commentator to display the harmony of Plato and Aristotle in most things.[26] Philoponus, who with his independent mind had thought better of his earlier belief in harmony, is castigated by Simplicius for neglecting this duty.[27]

The idea of harmony was extended beyond Plato and Aristotle to Plato and the Presocratics. Plato's pupils Speusippus and Xenocrates saw Plato as being in the Pythagorean tradition.[28] From the third to first centuries B.C., pseudo-Pythagorean writings present Platonic and Aristotelian doctrines as if they were the ideas of Pythagoras and his pupils,[29] and these forgeries were later taken by the Neoplatonists as genuine. Plotinus saw the Presocratics as precursors of his own views,[30] but Iamblichus went far beyond him by writing ten volumes on Pythagorean philosophy.[31] Thereafter Proclus sought to unify the whole of Greek philosophy by presenting it as a continuous clarification of divine revelation,[32] and Simplicius argued for the same general unity in order to rebut Christian charges of contradictions in pagan philosophy.[33]

Later Neoplatonist commentaries tend to reflect their origin in a teaching curriculum:[34] from the time of Philoponus, the discussion is often divided up into lectures, which are subdivided into studies of doctrine and of text. A general account of Aristotle's philosophy is prefixed to the *Categories* commentaries and divided, according to a formula of Proclus,[35] into ten questions. It is here that commentators explain the eventual purpose of studying Aristotle (ascent to the One) and state (if they do) the requirement of

[24] See Richard Sorabji, *Matter, Space and Motion* (London and Ithaca N.Y. 1988), ch. 15.

[25] See e.g. H.J. Blumenthal in n. 18 above.

[26] Simplicius *in Cat.* 7,23-32.

[27] Simplicius *in Cael.* 84,11-14; 159,2-9. On Philoponus' *volte face* see n. 21 above.

[28] See e.g. Walter Burkert, *Weisheit und Wissenschaft* (Nürnberg 1962), translated as *Lore and Science in Ancient Pythagoreanism* (Cambridge Mass. 1972), 83-96.

[29] See Holger Thesleff, *An Introduction to the Pythagorean writings of the Hellenistic Period* (Åbo 1961); Thomas Alexander Szlezák, *Pseudo-Archytas über die Kategorien*, Peripatoi vol. 4 (Berlin and New York 1972).

[30] Plotinus e.g. 4.8.1; 5.1.8 (10-27); 5.1.9.

[31] See Dominic O'Meara, *Pythagoras Revived: Mathematics and Philosophy in late Antiquity* (Oxford 1989).

[32] See Christian Guérard, 'Parménide d'Elée selon les Néoplatoniciens', forthcoming.

[33] Simplicius *in Phys.* 28,32-29,5; 640,12-18. Such thinkers as Epicurus and the Sceptics, however, were not subject to harmonisation.

[34] See the literature in n. 2 above.   [35] ap. Elian *in Cat.* 107,24-6.

displaying the harmony of Plato and Aristotle. After the ten-point introduction to Aristotle, the *Categories* is given a six-point introduction, whose antecedents go back earlier than Neoplatonism, and which requires the commentator to find a unitary theme or scope (*skopos*) for the treatise. The arrangements for late commentaries on Plato are similar. Since the Plato commentaries form part of a single curriculum they should be studied alongside those on Aristotle. Here the situation is easier, not only because the extant corpus is very much smaller, but also because it has been comparatively well served by French and English translators.[36]

Given the theological motive of the curriculum and the pressure to harmonise Plato with Aristotle, it can be seen how these commentaries are a major source for Neoplatonist ideas. This in turn means that it is not safe to extract from them the fragments of the Presocratics, or of other authors, without making allowance for the Neoplatonist background against which the fragments were originally selected for discussion. For different reasons, analogous warnings apply to fragments preserved by the pre-Neoplatonist commentator Alexander.[37] It will be another advantage of the present translations that they will make it easier to check the distorting effect of a commentator's background.

Although the Neoplatonist commentators conflate the views of Aristotle with those of Neoplatonism, Philoponus alludes to a certain convention when he quotes Plutarchus expressing disapproval of Alexander for expounding his own philosophical doctrines in a commentary on Aristotle.[38] But this does not stop Philoponus from later inserting into his own commentaries on the *Physics* and *Meteorology* his arguments in favour of the Christian view of Creation. Of course, the commentators also wrote independent works of their own, in which their views are expressed independently of the exegesis of Aristotle. Some of these independent works will be included in the present series of translations.

The distorting Neoplatonist context does not prevent the commentaries from being incomparable guides to Aristotle. The

---

[36] English: Calcidius *in Tim.* (parts by van Winden; den Boeft); Iamblichus fragments (Dillon); Proclus *in Tim.* (Thomas Taylor); Proclus *in Parm.* (Dillon); Proclus *in Parm.*, end of 7th book, from the Latin (Klibansky, Labowsky, Anscombe); Proclus *in Alcib. 1* (O'Neill); Olympiodorus and Damascius *in Phaedonem* (Westerink); Damascius *in Philebum* (Westerink); *Anonymous Prolegomena to Platonic Philosophy* (Westerink). See also extracts in Thomas Taylor, *The Works of Plato*, 5 vols. (1804). French: Proclus *in Tim.* and *in Rempublicam* (Festugière); *in Parm.* (Chaignet); Anon. *in Parm.* (P. Hadot); Damascius *in Parm.* (Chaignet).

[37] For Alexander's treatment of the Stoics, see Robert B. Todd, *Alexander of Aphrodisias on Stoic Physics* (Leiden 1976), 24-9.

[38] Philoponus *in DA* 21,20-3.

introductions to Aristotle's philosophy insist that commentators must have a minutely detailed knowledge of the entire Aristotelian corpus, and this they certainly have. Commentators are also enjoined neither to accept nor reject what Aristotle says too readily, but to consider it in depth and without partiality. The commentaries draw one's attention to hundreds of phrases, sentences and ideas in Aristotle, which one could easily have passed over, however often one read him. The scholar who makes the right allowance for the distorting context will learn far more about Aristotle than he would be likely to on his own.

The relations of Neoplatonist commentators to the Christians were subtle. Porphyry wrote a treatise explicitly against the Christians in 15 books, but an order to burn it was issued in 448, and later Neoplatonists were more circumspect. Among the last commentators in the main group, we have noted several Christians. Of these the most important were Boethius and Philoponus. It was Boethius' programme to transmit Greek learning to Latin-speakers. By the time of his premature death by execution, he had provided Latin translations of Aristotle's logical works, together with commentaries in Latin but in the Neoplatonist style on Porphyry's *Isagôgê* and on Aristotle's *Categories* and *de Interpretatione*, and interpretations of the *Prior* and *Posterior Analytics, Topics* and *Sophistici Elenchi*. The interruption of his work meant that knowledge of Aristotle among Latin-speakers was confined for many centuries to the logical works. Philoponus is important both for his proofs of the Creation and for his progressive replacement of Aristotelian science with rival theories, which were taken up at first by the Arabs and came fully into their own in the West only in the sixteenth century.

Recent work has rejected the idea that in Alexandria the Neoplatonists compromised with Christian monotheism by collapsing the distinction between their two highest deities, the One and the Intellect. Simplicius (who left Alexandria for Athens) and the Alexandrians Ammonius and Asclepius appear to have acknowledged their beliefs quite openly, as later did the Alexandrian Olympiodorus, despite the presence of Christian students in their classes.[39]

The teaching of Simplicius in Athens and that of the whole pagan Neoplatonist school there was stopped by the Christian Emperor Justinian in 529. This was the very year in which the Christian

[39] For Simplicius, see I. Hadot, *Le Problème du Néoplatonisme Alexandrin: Hiéroclès et Simplicius* (Paris 1978); for Ammonius and Asclepius, Koenraad Verrycken, *God en Wereld in de Wijsbegeerte van Ioannes Philoponus*, Ph.D. Diss. (Louvain 1985); for Olympiodorus, L.G. Westerink, *Anonymous Prolegomena to Platonic Philosophy* (Amsterdam 1962).

Philoponus in Alexandria issued his proofs of Creation against the earlier Athenian Neoplatonist Proclus. Archaeological evidence has been offered that, after their temporary stay in Ctesiphon (in present-day Iraq), the Athenian Neoplatonists did not return to their house in Athens, and further evidence has been offered that Simplicius went to Ḥarrān (Carrhae), in present-day Turkey near the Iraq border.[40] Wherever he went, his commentaries are a treasure house of information about the preceding thousand years of Greek philosophy, information which he painstakingly recorded after the closure in Athens, and which would otherwise have been lost. He had every reason to feel bitter about Christianity, and in fact he sees it and Philoponus, its representative, as irreverent. They deny the divinity of the heavens and prefer the physical relics of dead martyrs.[41] His own commentaries by contrast culminate in devout prayers.

Two collections of articles by various hands have been published, to make the work of the commentators better known. The first is devoted to Philoponus;[42] the second is about the commentators in general, and goes into greater detail on some of the issues briefly mentioned here.[43]

---

[40] Alison Frantz, 'Pagan philosophers in Christian Athens', *Proceedings of the American Philosophical Society* 119 (1975), 29-38; M. Tardieu, 'Témoins orientaux du *Premier Alcibiade* à Ḥarrān et à Nag 'Hammādi', *Journal Asiatique* 274 (1986); id., 'Les calendriers en usage à Ḥarrān d'après les sources arabes et le commentaire de Simplicius à la *Physique* d'Aristote', in I. Hadot (ed.), *Simplicius, sa vie, son oeuvre, sa survie* (Berlin 1987), 40-57; *Coutumes nautiques mésopotamiennes chez Simplicius*, in preparation. The opposing view that Simplicius returned to Athens is most fully argued by Alan Cameron, 'The last days of the Academy at Athens', *Proceedings of the Cambridge Philological Society* 195, n.s. 15 (1969), 7-29.

[41] Simplicius *in Cael.* 26,4-7; 70,16-18; 90,1-18; 370,29-371,4. See on his whole attitude Philippe Hoffmann, 'Simplicius' polemics', in Richard Sorabji (ed.), *Philoponus and the Rejection of Aristotelian Science* (London and Ithaca, N.Y. 1987).

[42] Richard Sorabji (ed.), *Philoponus and the Rejection of Aristotelian Science* (London and Ithaca, N.Y. 1987).

[43] Richard Sorabji (ed.), *Aristotle Transformed: the ancient commentators and their influence* (London and Ithaca, N.Y. 1990). The lists of texts and previous translations of the commentaries included in Wildberg, *Philoponus: Against Aristotle on the Eternity of the World* (pp.12ff.) are not included here. The list of translations should be augmented by: F.L.S. Bridgman, Heliodorus (?) in *Ethica Nicomachea*, London 1807.

I am grateful for comments to Henry Blumenthal, Victor Caston, I. Hadot, Paul Mercken, Alain Segonds, Robert Sharples, Robert Todd, L.G. Westerink and Christian Wildberg.